Link Baiting

**To improve your page
ranking on search engine**

Published in 2007 by
Corporate Turnaround Centre Pte Ltd.

Printed in Singapore
by Markono Print Media Pte Ltd.

9 8 7 6 5 4 3
09 08 07

Link Baiting

Table of Contents

Chapter Eight – Link Baiting Specialists

Chapter Nine – The Blogosphere

Chapter Ten – The Future of Link Baiting

Introduction to the Author

Dr Mike Teng is the author of the book *"Corporate Turnaround: Nursing a sick company back to health"*, in 2002 which is also trans lated into the Bahasa Indonesia. It was one of the top selling man agement books then. In 2006, he authored another book entitled, *"Corporate Wellness: 101 Principles in Turnaround and Transfor mation."* Both of these books are translated into Mandarin. He also published in 2007 three books, namely entitled:
Internet Turnaround: The Use of Intersnet Marketing to Turnaround Companies, Training Manual: Corporate Turnaround and Trans formation Methodology and Link Baiting to Improve Your Page Ranking on Search Engines.

He has been interviewed on the national media on many occasions on the subject of corporate turnaround and transformation. Dr Teng is widely recognized as a turnaround CEO in Asia by the news media such as the Channel NewsAsia, News Radio FM 93.8, the Boss Magazine, Economic Bulletin, the Today, World Executive Digest, Lianhe ZaoPao, StarBiz and the Straits Times.

Dr Teng is currently the Managing Director of a UK multinational company based in Singapore, responsible for the Asia Pacific region. He has 500 staff reporting into him.

He has 27 years of experience in corporate turnaround, strategic planning and operational management responsibilities in the Asia Pacific region. Of these, he held Chief Executive Officer's positions for 17 years in multi-national, local and publicly listed companies. He led in the successful turnaround of several troubled companies.

Dr Teng served as the Executive Council member for fourteen years and the last four years as the President of the Marketing Institute of Singapore (2000 - 2004), the national body representing individual and corporate members in Singapore. Dr Teng holds a Doctor in Business Administration (DBA) from the University of South Australia, Master in Business Administration (MBA) and Bachelor in Mechanical Engineering (BEng) from the National University of Singapore. He is also a Profes sional Engineer (P Eng, Singapore), Chartered Engineer (C Eng, UK) and Fellow Member of Chartered Institute of Marketing (FCIM), Chartered Management Institute (FCMI), Institute of Mechanical Engineers (FIMechE), Institute of Electrical Engi neers (FIEE), Marketing Institute of Singapore (FMIS) and Senior Member of Singapore Computer Society (SMSCS).

Introduction to the Author

Fione Tan is the President & CEO of **eOneNet.com**, with operations in Malaysia, Singapore and Hong Kong.

Fione is ranked the World's Top Internet Marketing Coach in top search engines. Her company, eOneNet.com, offers Internet Marketing consultancy, guaranteed SEO, search engines optimization, email marketing services and website business marketing training as well as internet marketing coaching.

Her company, eOneNet.com has also won many awards including the 2006 ZDNetAsia Top 50 IT companies in Asia Awards.

Fione is an international internet marketing speaker for various online marketing, business, entrepreneur development and women in business events in China, HK, Taiwan, Pakistan, Iran, UAE, India, Philippines, Thailand, Indonesia, Singapore and more.

Her clients range from home based entrepreneurs up to multinational corporations like Fuji Xerox, Apple, NEC, Goodyear and international banks.

Fione has been featured in numerous media and articles, including Business Times, The Star, News Straits Times, CompuTimes, The Sun, Malaysian Enterprise, Malaysian Business, The Edge Personal Money, Multimedia Malaysia, Jaring Internet Magazine, CNet, The Web, IT Malaysia, Female and Marie Claire magazine. She has also appeared on various segments regarding e-Business, such as Bloomberg News, CNBC Asia, Shanghai TV, Malaysia TV3, TV2, and Singapore Radio Station.

Full biodata in www.FioneTan.com and www.eOneNet.com

More info about her internet marketing blog can be found at www.eOneNet.com/internet_marketing_blog

Introduction to Link Baiting

'Link Baiting' is a new term that describes a relatively old concept; that is in terms of Internet age it has been around online for a number of years. Since the net exploded commercially, webmasters have been expanding their site's accessibility and market reach by attracting links from other sites. The idea is the more traffic you get the greater chance you have of increasing your bottom line and expanding your business's networks. Link baiting is the practice of producing something so useful, interesting, controversial, or valuable that people link to it. Link bait is essentially a hook. In many respects, it is the same concept as advertising. A good ad makes the viewer link back in their minds to a particular product or company associated with the ad. See the Gieco Insurance ads for more details. Cavemen and couples on reality television shows have very little to do with insurance. The point is not that the content of the ad relates to the product; the content is funny and thought provoking. Geico drop their name at the end. Everyone remembers Geico is an insurance company (and so they decide to use the service) because they can remember the funny ad. Link baiting is similar. If you put out good content – whether it's funny, thought-provoking, controversial, or just engaging – people will link back to you and thus you will build your online presence.

Link baiting is a term that encompasses many linking practices. The term itself first began appearing in SEO blogs in 2005. In the past 12 months the concept has emerged in mainstream Internet media as the latest trend in Internet marketing. The primary aim of any link bait is to increase the amount of incoming links to the company's sites. This can be done in a variety of ways, some more colorful and creative than others. Many experts believe that link baiting is merely good web sense and quality content, but within a medium that is in constant motion new techniques emerge everyday.

Professional Internet marketing can be the difference between success and failure.

Link baiting when successfully managed can be highly effective for not only generating new business but for brand promotion and exposure. For small to medium sized enterprises generating site traffic and opening the door to contemporary networks is paramount to holistic growth and development.

In the past year link bait has become the foremost marketing initiative for small to medium sized enterprises. Big corporations rely on big budgets and high visibility to drive traffic to their sites. SME's have to be more creative.

Link baiting can be a major driving force for rapid corporate turnaround.

The great thing about link baiting is that there is always something new on the horizon. Aside from traditional and proven methods of generating site traffic, there is new ground being uncovered everyday by Internet marketing and link baiting specialists.

A successful link baiting campaign will have two primary implications. The most significant short-term affect is the immediate insurgence of traffic. This can generate a substantial increase in business in a very short amount of time. Secondly your site will appear higher in the search engine rankings because of link popularity.

Search engine rankings are like goldmines for SMEs. If your site is ranking well your business is likely to be in good shape.

Simply put it can change the way you do business. A successful campaign will effectively reshape your business in terms of your growth, development and the all-important bottom line. Link baiting is the latest way to drive traffic to your site and to keep your visitors engaged. Overall link baiting means a complete overhaul of your businesses web presence and approach to Internet marketing. It is no longer about merely appealing to the search engines it is about a wider appeal. As search engines smarten up to new linking techniques it pays to be in the know and stay ahead of the game.

The most effective strategy for successfully increasing your link popularity is to construct a content rich, user friendly, optimized website which is regularly updated. If you can achieve those three things your links will come naturally and your visitors will be appropriate to your business. Link baiting is generally a referral to natural links however there is an element of manipulation in that the techniques are targeted and purposeful.

Overall the most important thing to remember about link baiting is that the term itself is a singular definition for a multitude of practices. It is hard to define such a broad range of ideas, concepts, tricks and techniques. One thing is for sure though; the next time you log onto the Internet these will have more than likely expanded. Internet marketing is in constant motion so keeping up with the practices is about understanding trends and moving with them. There is no one trick that will change the face of your business. The trick is understanding and knowledge. There are literally hundreds of tips and techniques available when it comes to link baiting the key is in knowing how to implement these into a successful and effective campaign.

The Origins of Link Baiting

Webmasters have been practicing link baiting for years. In fact for as long as the Internet has been a commercial marketing avenue link baiting has been a visible part of the equation. The term itself began to appear in the blogosphere in 2005. It began its rise into the mainstream in SEO blog circles. It is not clear who actually coined the term but its emergence can be accredited to blogger Nick Wilson and SEO expert Aaron Wall. Jim Westergren was also responsible for its rapid rise into SEM doctrine.

And so we come to Nick Wilson who is co-founder of Performancing.com, the worlds largest organization of professional bloggers. Since 2000, he has been involved in online publishing and community building. A lot of his work as a blogging expert is related to link baiting, a definite method of measuring the success of a blog. Like Nick Wilson, Aaron Wall can be looked upon as an authority on blogging and search engine optimization. He has plenty to say about both his website blog and www.seobook.com. Finally we have Jim Westergren, the CEO of SEO Fusion and world-renound expert in search engine optimization, online marketing, web development, and, of course, link baiting. The veritable "Big Three" of online viral marketing and, directly or indirectly, the inventors of link baiting.

Link baiting in the mainstream is largely due to the phenomenon of blogging. It actually began out of the desire to integrate communities. By linking to other blogs that were of similar content or interest, communities of like-minded individuals were formed. As the commercial potential of these communities and forums became apparent blogging increased and so did link baiting.

For many bloggers link bait was the only way for them to get their sites noticed. Link bait became a natural solution for marketing a site or blog. As the phenomenon exploded into the mainstream so too did the SEO blogs that we were talking. This is really where the term came into prominence. Expert SEO and Internet marketers began talking about the implications of link baiting in mainstream marketing.

Besides blogging, another great method of marketing, generating links to your site, is to develop a strategic video. Optimize YouTube and drive video traffic from YouTube to your site. That is the basic principle. The best kind of videos – and online videos are really catching on – is one that either has shock value or oddball humor. Shock or titillate your audience and you almost guarantee they will come back.

The so-called "shoes" video apparently ranks because it's a viral hit. Because of the nature of social networking, particularly as it now taps into video marketing, you might also be able to successfully market your company with a YouTube hit. The easiest, cheapest, fastest and perhaps cleverest way is to get your users to make it for you.

The idea of link bait can be linked to viral marketing. Link bait is a hook and the aim is for it to spread. The potential for mass distribution of link bait is huge on the Internet. This is partially why link baiting can be so successful. One link on the right site or blog could expose your site to millions.

Link bait moved away from other more traditional forms of linking in that it was considered purely organic. It was a natural form of generating links and a concept works because it's simple. Give people what they want, give them something to talk about or something they can use. This will create natural links. As link bait becomes a more recognized concept it becomes apparent that users are not the only ones to benefit. Search engines use link popularity to access a sites relevance and importance in relation to key search words. This is a huge plus for search engine rankings. A good ranking can truly enhance site potential and the increased traffic creates the opportunity for more back links

Modern link baiting is a little less natural and a bit more creative. Link baiting campaigns are driven, viral marketing attempts that can boost the health of your business with a single bit of bait. It is sometimes hard to distinguish between natural content development and link bait attempts. It is true most webmasters are developing their sites with link baiting in mind but there is also more consideration going towards users. That is the great thing about link bait. It forces webmasters to hook their visitors with something of use. Overall this enhances the entire web experience.

Link Baiting Basics (Link Baiting vs Backlinks?)

The basic aim of a piece of link bait is to attract traffic to a site in order to secure backlinks. Backlinks are incoming links from other pages. Back links are valuable because links are the fundamental connectors of the Internet. They are the navigation system used by both search engines and web users. The more links you have pointing to a site the greater the potential audience. Link bait is targeted at that potential audience of traffic.

The number of backlinks is an indication of the popularity and user-rated importance of a website or specific webpage. A backlink is any link received by a web page, website directory, or website domain from another web page, site directory, or domain. They are sometimes called incoming links, inbound links, inlinks, and inward links.

What makes backlinks an important: major search engines' feature is to look at a website's number of backlinks. This will help determine a website's search engine ranking. Google's PageRank algorithms use backlinks and as Google is one of the leading search engines, it is very advantageous to have a lot of backlinks to get a high ranking.

Most commercial search engines let users see the number of backlinks they have recorded to a particular web page. Google can be searched using link to find the number of pages linked to it but bear in mind that Yahoo!'s Site Explorer and Microsoft's Windows Live Search may give more accurate backlink counts.

Link bait generates two kinds of specific traffic. The first is traffic via click through links. This is known as direct traffic and can be useful for growing your business and increasing link popularity. The other way in which traffic is driven to your site via linking is through search engine optimization. This in essence is making your site more search engine friendly in order to increase your ranking. Sites that are search engine friendly are usually user-friendly too. Link popularity is a major consideration for search engine rankings.

Link baiting can be performed in many ways, some simple, and others more complex and costly. Link baiting is essentially about selling your site as useful, interesting or noteworthy. It's about getting people through the virtual door and giving them a reason to want to come back or spread the word about your site. Link baiting is also about converting those visitors into incoming links.

The definition of link baiting encompasses both new and old techniques. Traditional forms of link bait aligned with SEO. More contemporary link bait is a little harder to put in a box. When you are getting started it is useful to look at some of the most basic ways you can generate back links.

Basic Baiting

- Content quality – This is the most basic and can be the most effective way to increase your link popularity. By populating your site with great content you are drawing people in and giving them a reason to link to you. Content quality can be a major factor in corporate turnaround. It is the foundation of any successful link baiting marketing strategies. This is the most basic baiting technique in the book.

- Web directory submissions –A manual form of baiting links but the result will be natural linking. Submitting your site to web directories promotes visibility and exposure. Once you are in the mix, you'll be generating traffic and hooking visitors to your site. There are paid directories and unpaid directories, all of which showcase your site. Industry-specific directories generally drive the best traffic to your site.

- Web content article submissions are free and paid services – This is one of the most common methods for generating links. You can submit articles to a variety of sites both, paid and unpaid and links will be made through content. This is a great way to generate click. By submitting quality articles to these directories, you make your site very visible. If your articles are being read and if they are useful you will get a lot of links. The best example of an article submission site is www.digg.com.

- Hosting articles– Search engines love sites changing their content; sites that have a high-content-turnover. That said, articles written to be keyword rich and search engine optimized are not generally the best. Articles written for readers, visitors to your site, are definitely the best. Search engines pick up on articles loaded with keywords. It's getting harder to have these types of articles picked up as engines become more discriminatory:. You are better off to provide valuable keyword optimized information articles on your site. Quality far outdoes quantity: information rich, concise articles are the best option. You can create your own resource section and fill it with articles or offer to host other authors on your site.

- Tools and resources – If you can create a useful tool or general resource on your website, you are sure to increase backlinks as it is picked up. The type of tool doesn't essentially matter; it can be amusing, interesting, useful, or all three. If you create something new and specific to your industry or product, you are a step ahead of the game. Resources generate quality backlinks and get your users talking.

Good, effective link baiting is ongoing process but its value in terms of Internet marketing is priceless. If you can establish your site in the rankings or develop something unique and useful, you will have a constant stream of traffic. The more traffic you generate the more business you will acquire.

The basic notion of link baiting is that good content speaks for itself. The aim is to create something worthwhile and useful so that people will link to your site. Good content is worthwhile and useful so all you need to know is how to optimize that content. Many experts believe that good content alone will serve as sufficient link bait. **However fate sometimes needs a little push in the right direction.**

The Purpose of Link Baiting

A link bait is an element of website content designed to attract attention from an extended audience of traffic. Attention equates to traffic; traffic leads to links and back links. Increasing traffic is the main aim of any SEO or link baiting campaign. The more people you connect with, the more businesses you connect with, the more hits and business opportunities you secure. Link baiting is about finding ways to draw potential clients or customers to your site. Although methods and practices vary the central idea remains the same: whatever you do, your link baiting should drive traffic to your site.

The ideal content for link baiting has a viral effect. That is, it spreads like wild-fire. One person passes in on to another, and they pass it on to another. The purpose of link baiting content is designed to spread. The Internet is a powerful medium. Its potential for distributing new information is immense and virtually unprecedented. Once the content is out there, it is global within seconds, and if it is good then the influx of traffic can be astronomical.

Webmasters continue to develop some colorful ways to spread content online and maximize link possibilities. As a general rule, entertaining content will be quickly picked up and ultimately becomes available anywhere online. Content that tends to be picked up quickly includes news, controversy, articles, tools or software to name a few. Web publishers and users link to the content. If it's helpful to them or their visitors, you have a sure-fire way of directing a lot of traffic to your site.

Link baiting is ideal for small to medium sized enterprises that may not be in a field that allows a lot of linking opportunity. The purpose of link baiting is to get other sites to link to you therefore expanding your potential market. For SME's link baiting can be a great way to improve site rankings. The idea is to create something that will generate a lot of attention. Generating interest is the oldest trick in the marketing book and the more creative the better. If you can come up with something new then you are on to a winner. This can be difficult to do when it comes to online marketing however you might already be heading in the right direction without even knowing it.

So why bother going to all the trouble? Let us look at the possible outcomes of a successful link baiting campaign. For a small to medium sized enterprise marketing is fundamental to success.

There are thousands of tried and true ways to market a website. The problem is that search engines recognise these traditional tricks and audiences are craving something new.

Marketing is about appealing to a targeted audience. Link baiting is about attracting not only targeted audiences but also expanded demographics of people. The thing about the Internet is that all you need is one great idea and you could potentially reach millions of people. The purpose of link bait may not be to reach millions of new users but a few specific industry related ones.

There are a lot of ways to bait people to link to your site. If you have good content then you are properly already doing it without even knowing. A driven purposeful campaign however takes a little more effort. If you can create a hook such as a news item that is fresh off the press, a useful download, something new, useful or informative you will get people linking to your site.

Once you have the hook you can sit back and watch the traffic roll in and your ranking rise. Whatever that hook may be, if it takes off you will see results within 24 hours. An example of this is breaking news. If you can be one of the first to post breaking news or information on your site, you will immediately increase your sites ranking. If you manage to get it out there quickly when a person searches the engines for the story your site will be up there. Once you have them through the door there is a good chance they will link to your site so that they can share the information.

One significant consideration with link baiting is that unlike industry specific content link bating content is universal. This means that your content is not solely industry related but globally appealing. Link baiting content should be memorable and valuable to diverse groups.

The purpose of a link bait campaign is to stir up interest in your site or services. Linking connects communities and creates an environment for interaction. Link bait can help position your brand within your community in a way that you may have struggled to do before.

Where to start

If you go to a search engine and type in the keywords link baiting or link popularity you will literally be bombarded by hundreds of thousands of hits. This overload of information can be hard to decipher leaving you wondering where to start. The link baiting explosion has seen the emergence of a multitude of so called experts claiming to know all the tricks of the trade. The truth is this is new ground for many webmasters and SEO experts. Everyday there is something new being developed to generate links.

The best trick when you are starting out is to keep it simple. Link baiting can be complicated and time consuming but it doesn't have to be. For small to medium sized enterprises the most effective way to build link popularity is through strong content. This is content such as articles, reviews, reports and news. SME's need should concentrate on a holistic approach to increasing link popularity.

Content is a good place to start any link baiting campaign. You can write about anything but content that is related to your business and your customers will be best for SEO purposes. Strong content is the most pure form of link bait. Populate your site with quality information, relevant resources and newsworthy plugs and you will generate links. Your content is your hook; it is what makes your site unique and attracts visitors. Once you have them hooked the rest is easy.

Once you have a site that is worth visiting you need to get the word out there to the general web public. Begin by submitting your site to relevant directories. Think globally as well as locally and hit the big directories. Directories are a great way to get your site on the map but there is also a risk that your link will get lost in the crowd. The best kinds of links are those that are embedded in content. Article directories also give you linking opportunities.

Content links are simple and effective for creating incoming traffic and increasing your ranking. Submit articles to directories related to your industry. This gives you prime opportunity to add links into the content. You can also offer your articles to sites free providing they add a link to your site. This is a great way of promoting your site and creating a click through. Again related sites are best for generating actual business.

Blogs are a great way to generate interest and backlinks. They are simple to manage and cost effective. Blogs are ideal for link baiting because blogging communities are so well integrated. Become an interactive member of a blogging community and use your connections to generate links. Linking to other blogs is a good way to create some link love for yourself.

Another simple way to create an opportunity for linking is to create interest pages on your site. Ideally this will be information or news of interest to your customers. If you can get in early or present some news worthy or new information you will generate buzz. Buzz equals links and link popularity. This is also a great way to get your site in the top ten.

Getting started is often hard simply because the wealth of information out there is so overwhelming. To begin with, stick to simple proven avenues for linking. From there you can expand and get more creative as you learn more about what your customers want from your site.

You can check the progress of your campaign using service such as Marketleap or PageRank. Using this type of service you can track the number of incoming links and your ranking.

CHAPTER TWO – SEARCH ENGINE OPTIMIZATION

Understanding Search Engines

To fully optimize your business' web potential you need to understand the ins and outs of search engines. Search engines rank websites based on a number of things. This will vary depending on the search engine but the basic principles are the same for all. Knowing how to get the most out of a search engine will significantly increase your chances of a good ranking. A good ranking is anything inside the top 20, a great ranking is top 10.

When you type in keywords the search engine performs an index search. That is it scans through its own pages and comes up with the results according to what it has in its database. The database is made up of sites that have been submitted to the search engine and sites that have been automatically scanned by the engines crawler or spider. A search engines crawler scans the web for sites to add to its index so that it can present the most relevant results for its users.

Search engine's concentrate on a number of key factors to decide on the sites ranking.

- Keywords

Keywords are very important for search engines. When a search is performed the keywords in the sites content are what the engine matches to the search words. The search engine takes into consideration the density and placement of keywords to determine relevance and ranking. Search engines are keyword smart in that they will not be fooled by keyword overload or content that is totally designed as search engine bait.

- Link popularity

Search engines calculate the amount of incoming links generated by a particular page. The links will be more effective if they are relevant to the sites content and to the business. Search engines often overlook links to random unrelated sites. Links to credible recognizable sites will have a more significant impact on the search engines analysis of your incoming links. Search engines look at incoming links to determine the relevancy of your sites content to the search.

- Content

Good content is invaluable when it comes to search engine rankings. A page with well placed keyword rich; valuable content will rank high in the results. Pages with pointless content that doesn't make sense to readers will not be effective in increasing your ranking. Content that is useful, informative and that references key terms will catch the search engines crawler.

- SE friendly design

Search engines crawl sites top to bottom so design is important. You want the search engine to be able to access your content quickly and easily. Flash headers and banners push content down the page and detract from the impact of your keywords. Stick to simple, clean and user friendly designs with minimal heavy coding.

- Meta tags

Title tags are important for search engines as they give a description of the content within the site. Meta tags are considered useful for SEO but these days other avenues have become apparent. It is still important however to have clean, precise tags that describe the content of the site. For each page uses a different title tag.

In this section, the introduction to search engines and search engine optimization, is modified from content posted byAaron Wall on his SEOBook.com website. The tips give you a rich, comprehensive introduction to SEO in terms of how you can actually benefit from it...what you need to do. Here goes:

- You don't have to spend lots of money on SEO for your website if you are willing to work hard and if you try hard to come up with unique, <u>creative,</u> and useful ideas.

- You can look at what your competitors are doing to get attention on the search engines but it is hard to catch up with a competitor if you only follow their foot steps.

- It's always a better plan to develop new strategies or integrate a variety of strategies from different markets to boost your SEO performance.

- Viral marketing is huge.

- Most SEO tools sold online are a waste of time and money. Most of them are outdated and emphasize the wrong area of focus. They encourage people to think about arbitrary goals instead of about logical holistic marketing methods and social interaction.

- Success takes time.

- If you can afford it, <u>buying an old site</u> is a good way to start if you're competing on Google in a saturated market.

- Older sites seem to be able to get away with more "gray area" things than a new site can.

- Sometimes buying a custom ad page on a trusted site is the cheapest and quickest way to the top of keyword search results.

- Google is tough. They only want to count legitimate editorial citations; no paid ads

- MSN and Yahoo! are still pretty easy to manipulate using link spam.

- There are still many arbitrage opportunities and unexplored categories.

- The web is like New York City: there is so much demand, implied intent, and capital that even small niches can become highly profitable if you target your site and brand around them.

- Duplicate content filters are getting better.

- Human <u>editorial</u> <u>review</u> is an important part of all major search engines. .

- It is easy to get burned out or feel like you are stuck in a hole so do something you're truly interested in; it will make you less likely to burn out.

Understanding SEO and Marketing

Search engine optimization is key for SME's. The best way to get people to your site is by appearing in the top ten results. How many times do you go past the top ten? It's a sad but true fact that many sites with great content will never get seen simply because they don't know how to optimize their site for search engines.

SEO can be looked at as holistic approach to building and maintaining a site. From the design to the coding to the content, a site must be search engine friendly. Let us look at the elements that make up a site and what you can do to ensure they are working for you.

- Design

Getting the web site design right is essential. If you have a look around the Internet you will find dazzling, exciting and innovative sites. You will also find static, simplistic and somewhat dull sites. Which is best for a SEO? Somewhere in between is ideal for SEO for a number of reasons. Search engines scan the coding from top to bottom. Flash designs, elaborate navigation and drop down menus push your content down the page. Ideally you want the search engine to be able to access your content and its keywords easily.

On the other hand while a static simple design is easier for the search engine it is less appealing to audiences. The more traffic you get to your site the more likely you will have people linking to you. Search engines assess link popularity and if your site is dull, people are not going to want to come back no matter how good the information is.

So the middle ground is something clean, professional and appealing to both search engines and audiences. A little creativity with design goes a long way but it is best to keep it simple. Web design experts are well equipped to help you find the right combination of style and SEO

- Content

When it comes to content the more you have the better. Quality content is your greatest tool in attracting search engine rankings. Quality content also leads to link baiting which is great for your ranking too. Apart from basic content upgrades there are a lot of ways you can attract high rankings. Articles, reviews and news are just a few ways in which you can increase the content on your site. The content should be valuable and informative with the focus on providing resources for your visitors. Search engines recognize content that does not fulfil these criteria. Your content can be packed with keywords in a way that works for audiences as well as search engines. Newsletters and ezines are also great ways to increase the content on your site and to attract page views.

- Tools

Useful tools or downloads have a dual effect on your site. Firstly they are great for your users; they provide a reason to come back to your site. Secondly if they are coming back then they are likely to link to you. Incoming links are imperative for SEO. Creating a tool that people find useful will generate a lot of incoming traffic and links. This will ultimately increase your rankings.

Finally there are a number of ways to look at SEO in the context of your own website. There are two binary methods labeled 'white hat' and 'black hat'. 'White hat' methods are that of building content and improving site usefulness and quality. These are approved by search engines as natural ways to building site rankings. 'Black hat' methods are a little more manipulative. These methods include tricking search engines using cloaking techniques or spamming. There are conflicting views from both sides however 'white hat' appears to be the more productive way of SEO.

Black Hat and White Hat Marketing

When it comes to the Internet there are a world of ways in which you can market your business and your site. Some of these ways are search engine approved while others are more underhanded. SEO marketing falls in to two categories: Black Hat and White Hat. These terms are used to define what is considered good marketing practice and bad marketing practice.

White hat SEO is about working within the search engines guidelines to achieve optimization. This means using techniques that are search engine approved such as improving the content and quality of a site. White hat SEO marketing is about providing strong content and promoting user experience whilst remaining within the search engine guidelines. Search engines encourage webmasters to optimize their site with users in mind and make it easy for the search engines spider or crawler. This means ensuring content is targeted towards users and the site is technically optimized for the search engine. Technical optimization includes clean and simple design practices, clear concise coding, strong links, short download times, effective navigation structure.

White hat methods include:

- Providing valuable, informative, quality content that addresses audience interests.
- Replacing wordy, indeterminate page content with specific relevant terms.
- Optimizing Meta tags with accurate concise page descriptions.
- Giving each page its own unique title tag.
- Optimizing keywords with relevant research driven words and phrases
- Optimizing design so that the crawler can access your sites content more easily.
- Creating articles and resources that are of use to your visitors.
- Creating viable link bait.
- Ensuring site usability by eliminating broken links, heavy download and complicated navigation.
- Increase site accessibility by ensuring the anchor tag hyperlinks are operating for all pages.
- Allowing easy access to spiders or crawlers.

Black hat techniques are considered by many webmasters to be a form of manipulation. These methods include fooling the search engine with cloaking techniques, spam and other negative practices. These are not approved marketing methods and while they may produce results they are not recommended. Black hat methods are those that are not approved by search engines and that will therefore result in reduced ranking or exclusion from the search engines index. These methods are considered deceptive and unproductive because they focus solely on search engine manipulation without regard for their users.

Black hat methods:

- Spamming is the practice of overloading keywords to increase site ranking. This results in irrelevant site exposure so that the site will be appearing in results where it has little relevance to the search and user.
- Spamdexing is the practice of promoting a site pages through deceptive manipulation of search algorithms. This is a common black hat method for gaining exposure for commercial pages.

- Cloaking is when the search engine is presented with an optimized page to boost that ranking then the users are presented with a different less relevant version of the page.

There are many opposing views when it comes to the idea of white and black hat SEO marketing. Advocates of black hat methods say that all forms of SEM are about manipulating the search engine rankings. White hat supporters believe that black hat methods are deceptive, underhanded and unethical. Search engines support this view and where black hat methods are detected action will be taken. A number of big brand sites have been excluded from indexes for abusing the search engine systems with black hat techniques.

In recent years the lines between white hat and black hat SEO have gotten slightly blurred. Many strictly white hat webmasters have found themselves delving into black hat SEO simply because their sites were going unnoticed. So where is the line? Life is not as simple as black and white and neither is SEM. The line falls between ethical and unethical SEM practices but there are definitely shades of gray. There are those that follow search engine rules and guidelines (white hat) and those that don't (black hat). That is simple enough but how do you know where the line is if you can't see it?

The main points of difference between white hat and black hat techniques are:

- Content

White hat content is created for the user as well as the search engine whereas black hat content is specifically designed to attract the search engine. Black hat content is often overloaded with keywords and of very poor quality with no use to the reader. White hat content is made for the user so the experience is a lot more positive.

- Quality

White hat sites are typically of better quality holistically. White hat SEM is about catering to the search engine as though it was just another visitor. This generally means that the site will be clean, well populated and relevant. Black hat sites make the mistake of forgetting about their visitors often populating sites with incoherent content.

- SEO

White hat methods should not cause problems with search engines. If you follow the guidelines and stick to good practices the search engine will be a friend not a foe. For black hat marketing professionals it is a constant battle with the search engine.

- Results

In the short term black hat methods may increase traffic and business. However white hat techniques are about long-term results that convert not only into traffic but growth and development.

SEO and Link Baiting

For SME's a high search engine ranking is like money in the bank. It means a huge number of prospects coming along to the site; it's free advertising to rank high on Google based on the popularity of your site, free organic marketing. Internet marketing is about creating credibility, appealing to audiences and increasing traffic. This is often difficult online due to the sheer number of competitors. Having your site appear high in the search engine rankings generates credibility as well as hits. So it goes without saying that building your ranking and optimizing your site for search engine success is very important.

SEO is a side effect of good link baiting. If your site is being linked to then chances are your ranking will be significantly affected. The impact of good link baiting on your ranking provides both short and long-term benefits. In the short term a viral baiting campaign could see your site inside the top 25 within 24 hours. This bodes well for the future of your site and your ranking. Once a person has linked to your site they are inclined to come back. They are also inclined to spread the word. This means that your ranking will remain high and your audience will expand as you sit back and watch the page views grow.

The more incoming links you have the better your ranking will be. Many search engines consider how many links you have going to your site and its individual pages when ranking your site. The number of links you have is important, as is the quality of the sites that are linking to yours. It comes back to the basic idea of credibility. The aim is to increase link popularity via quality industry specific site linking.

The best way to increase your search engine ranking via link baiting is to create something worth linking to. Good content will get people through the door and keep them coming back. Great content will encourage people to spread the word.

These days it seems like everyone is trying to increase their rankings by increasing link popularity. Link popularity is something that is checked by many search engines when ranking sites. The search engine considers sites with incoming links from quality related sites to be more desirable. This means that some major search engines might overlook random links and viral linking. Most major search engines will boost the rankings of sites with a high number of quality incoming links. A high number of incoming links presents a site as desirable, useful and informative.

Link quality is very important to SEO. This means that while your site might have a high number of incoming links they might not be considered quality. The best kinds of links for your ranking come from related sites, quality credible directories and well-known webmasters, bloggers or writers.

Content is key when talking in terms of search engine rankings and link popularity. The more content you have on your site the more likely you are to get incoming links. Articles are a great way to increase your ranking and build links. By having a content rich site you encourage your visitors to link back to you and you give the search engine plenty to consider. Expanding your content opens up doors to link popularity and gives you the opportunity to take your site to the next level.

The advantages of this include

- More pages for the search engine to index when ranking your site.
- Greater opportunity for reciprocal linking.
- Opportunity for web site and credibility promotion.
- The ability to present yourself as a leading expert.
- You will be providing visitors with content that is relevant and useful to them.
- You can promote your site ranking with keyword rich pages.

Search Engine Optimization Basics – Important Questions?

What is your submission doing for you?

When submitting to directories think about which sites are best and how your link is going to be displayed. A link on a page amongst hundreds of others is not going to do you any favors. Links embedded in valuable content are best. Submit your site to credible, recognized directories. Your submission could be pointless if you get it wrong. Site submissions are about promoting visibility so make sure your directory is visible within your market.

What kinds of sites are you linking to?

It's best to stick to ones, which are related to your industry. Non related links are often by passed by search engines where as related links not only provide traffic they are also great for widening your networks. Trade links with sites that you find useful and credible. Outgoing links are a great way to attract incoming ones so link to sites you might like a back link from.

Is your content useful, informative and audience driven?

Gone are the days of overloaded keyword articles and cramming code with tags and phrases. Search engines are smart and the best kind of content for your ranking is well written and information rich. Keywords are still important but good content will attract back links as well as increase your ranking.

Is your site and content optimized for usability?

Usability is a buzzword that means improving user experience. When it comes to optimizing your site this is an essential element. If you can predict what your users want and give it to them then you are optimizing your site for both search engine and linking success. When it comes to usability consider design, navigation, content and speed.

Are natural links enough?

Link baiting is considered a natural way to increase your link popularity however organic links are often complemented nicely by purposeful linking techniques. The idea with link baiting is that people will naturally link to a site because the content is useful, interesting, funny or newsworthy. Increasing your sites content and improving its appeal will create natural links. Adding tools, news sections, podcasts, reviews and interviews to your site repertoire will significantly add to your link popularity.

What kinds of sites should you be trying to bait links from?

The best kinds of sites are the ones that are related to your industry. These sites complement your business and customers. Search engines look at link popularity to determine how important and relevant a page is to the performed search. If you have a lot of incoming links from sites that are recognized in your community it will boost your ranking.

What are the options for link trading?

Trading links is a great way to boost your link popularity and optimize your site for search engine success. Establish some reciprocal linking opportunities within your community. Trade links with sites that will make your site look more credible. You can swap links with affiliates, contemporaries or complementary sites. This is considered a gray area in terms of link baiting as it is not a natural form of attracting links. However it is considered part of link baiting strategies and techniques.

CHAPTER THREE – INTERNET MARKETING

The Evolution of Internet Marketing

The Internet in its inception was initially used solely as an information network medium for sending emails and sharing files. Its growth and literal explosion in the mid 1990s was due largely to its commercialization. The Internet as we know it today, a super highway of information, commerce, interconnectivity and expression began as a small collection of static product pages. The Internet was a new marketing avenue for businesses to expose their products to a larger audience.

The eventual commercial growth of the Internet superseded all expectations; the development of the Internet as a social network also exceeded its primary vision. The Internet as we know it today was born out of commercial marketing. More and more businesses saw the Internet as a viable avenue for marketing products. Static pages were quickly upgraded with graphics, navigation systems and links. Next came the ability to buy and sell online. This is where the market really began to boom. Nowadays it's as simple as clicking a mouse and you can buy practically anything online.

As more and more people joined the .com buzz it quickly became apparent that simply having a website is not enough. The concept of marketing websites in order to market products and services emerged. From very early on webmasters have been finding new and interesting ways to attract visitors to their sites and increase their search engine rankings.

Internet marketing nowadays is a booming industry. There is nothing more important for webmasters than marketing, as without it you will be virtually invisible. Basic marketing techniques that emerged early on included trying to increase search engine rankings. This progressed into SEO or SEM. Search engine optimization is on the top of every webmasters list when it comes to increasing rankings and therefore traffic. The aim is always top ten. SEO encompasses all the elements of a site. From design, layout, content and coding to link popularity and usability.

SEO quickly became the focus of marketing campaigns net wide and with this many theories emerged as to how to achieve optimization. Usability is an important marketing concept that got a lot of attention in the early days of SEO. The concept of usability is all about enhancing user experience and ensuring that the user is able to access relevant, specific information in a simple and effective manner. Usability concepts have implications for design, content, navigation and all other site elements. This idea generally requires a lot of market research and the site is tailored towards targeted users. These concepts work well for SEO purposes as search engines rank sites geared towards users well.

The latest in Internet marketing news is the concept of link baiting. This has been around since the inception of commercialized business online, but the term is under a year old. Link bait is anything on a site that inspires a user to link to the site. It can be something useful, funny, silly, controversial or newsworthy. Anything that attracts natural links is considered link bait. Linking baiting is an important tool in the SEO arsenal as search engines rate link popularity.

Essentially Internet marketing is changing all the time. New concepts, tricks and techniques emerge everyday. It is important however to remember that although Internet marketing is constantly evolving the basic principal of marketing always remains the same. The audience is everything, the market is key.

Understanding Internet Marketing

If you are new to marketing then the world of Internet marketing can be somewhat overwhelming. In fact even if you are experienced you may still feel a little unsure of where to start when it comes to online marketing. Firstly remember the normal rules do not apply.

Internet marketing is as changeable as the weather. If you are looking to research the subject online then be prepared to be bombarded with 'experts' trying to sell you their services. On the Internet anyone can claim to be an expert. Be prepared for an overwhelming number of results that may contradict each other to the point where you are so confused you might buy anything.

The truth is the subject of Internet marketing is so vast and variable it seems impossible to keep up. The normal rules do not apply when you talking about Internet marketing but the basic principals of marketing do. The fundamental marketing principal you need to remember is market focus. The best thing you can do in terms of marketing your site is to remember whom you are marketing to. All too often in the world of Internet marketing people get lost trying to trick the search engines, spam the market or overdo their campaign. Sure these techniques might get people to your site but when they get there what do they find?

The best way to ensure your site reaches a lot of people is to create content that is worthwhile, useful and usable. A number of years ago the concept of usability emerged as the latest and greatest in new wave Internet marketing. The idea was based around making your site user friendly. This means ensuring whoever visits your site has a positive experience. Usability explored the concepts of design, navigation and content. Looking for ways in which these things could be refined so that users had a flawless experience. Usability can also be interpreted as the process of making your site search engine friendly. Often the two can go hand in hand.

The concept of usability has been somewhat overshadowed by new advancements in search engine attraction. For anyone trying to market their site, especially SME's, getting a high ranking is key to success. But why move away from the idea of making your site a place for your customers? Its simple you don't have to. These days search engines are smart and a site that is built for its users will rank higher in the results than one that is using all the tricks in the book. Good content, useful information and user experience goes a long way towards increasing your sites rankings. Good content is ultimately what both the search engine and the audience want.

So how do you compete with the giants using all the latest tricks in the Internet marketing book? Simple, you don't. The best way to get your site ranked is to be unique. Create information that only you can create, offer content that is new and fresh that no body else has. If you follow all the basic principals of usability when designing and constructing your site, set yourself up as an expert with great content and send out feelers for links, you will enjoy the results.

The key to Internet marketing just like traditional marketing is to know your market, target your audience and give them what they want. That is a surefire why to ensure that once you get them to your site they are going to come back for more.

So what's the latest in Internet marketing? Link baiting. This is a new term to define an old concept. Link baiting is an increasingly effective tool and can have a significant impact if managed correctly. Link baiting is all about getting people to link to your site. They might do so because you have useful information, news or some kind of tool. There are many reasons a person might link to your site naturally however it doesn't hurt to tip the odds in your favor.

Link baiting is a spin off of good quality content and for those in the business of increasing their rankings it is something search engines will look for. The key is linking with sites that are relevant or complementary to your business. This bodes well in the search engines assessment of your sites relevancy. You want the sites that link to you to be credible also. If you have credible related sites linking to your site the search engine is going to look favorably upon your site.

There are 101 Internet marketing tricks that might very well get your site in the top ten. However the best trick is having something worth selling. You may get people through the door with gimmicks and gadgets but if in the end there is nothing useful to keep them coming back or to get them to link to you then the results are only short term. Internet marketing is about appealing to the search engines as well as the audience.

Internet Marketing and Corporate Turnaround

When talking in terms of marketing strategies for SME's the Internet is the number one avenue for corporate turnaround. The Internet is an opportunity to reinvent strategies, branding and holistically give your company the edge over its competitors. The beauty of Internet marketing for SME's is that the Internet has limitless marketing potential.

Small to medium sized businesses are especially susceptible to changes within the market both locally and globally. This places these businesses at risk because fluctuations in the market have such a huge impact. What if you could change all that by simply changing the angle of your approach? Internet marketing is all about how you approach your audiences, what you have to offer and how you communicate that. The Internet is a communication medium so it's imperative that you understand that every aspect of your site is communicating a message to your potential clientele.

What does your site say about your business? More importantly how does it communicate what you can do for your customers? This is the most important part of your marketing campaign online. Web users scan pages almost in the same way search engines do. They are looking for relevant information and they want to be able to access it quickly and easily. Your visitors want to know exactly what you can do for them and they want to find out in less than 3 clicks.

Have you ever wondered why your business is not generating as much online revenue as you hope? You won't have to look far to discover the reasons behind this. Your website is the window to your business. Generally if your window is dirty your customers won't look beyond that. So the first step to turning around your business is getting the marketing right. Refine your branding and cultivate your image. Clean up your window and show your customers what you can do for them.

Internet marketing is the essential ingredient in major corporate turnaround. The idea of corporate turnaround is not just about making your business more appealing and accessible it is about working from the inside out, taking a holistic approach to marketing. Many Internet marketing campaigns concentrate too extensively on SEO experts, merely scratching the surface of your problems but not really effecting significant change. If you approach marketing from a holistic viewpoint the long-term results will be notable. Internet marketing is more than SEO. Sure this is a big part of the process but realistically SEO will happen naturally if you get the initial phases of marketing right.

The important thing to remember is that not all experts are created equal. There are those that claim to be able to turn your business around but are only talking about the superficial areas. Real corporate turnaround experts take a deeper view of the health of your business. These experts are equipped to manage the marketing of your business from a holistic standpoint. This means that you get the complete overhaul not just the quick fix version. This kind of approach really works best for SME's as they have the potential to go either way. SME's are affected by subtle changes in the market in the same way they are also influenced by subtle changes to their own infrastructure. This means that of all business types they are most responsive to change

Viral Marketing and Link Baiting

Link baiting is a marriage of traditional viral marketing and new wave popular tech. Link bait is a hook for viral marketing, an attempt to reach an extensive portion of the market in a short amount of time. No where has viral marketing been more effective than on the Internet. The impact of a link baiting or an online viral marketing campaign is dependent on the amount of links generated by the campaign. On the Internet, links can spread like a virus, invading every inch of the network within hours. This kind of marketing takes traditional viral marketing to a new level.

In essence traditional viral marketing and link baiting have a lot in common. The aim of both viral marketing and link bait is to spread. The primary goals of link baiting include increasing traffic, promoting brand visibility and increasing rankings. Online viral marketing aims to increase link popularity. Link popularity will convert into increased traffic, visibility and rankings

The potential for link bait to have a viral effect is high if you can come up with a great hook. It's easy to see how one link can turn in thousands in a very short space of time. Information is spread across the global community via links and backlinks. Unlike traditional viral marketing, link baiting can literally turn your campaign globally in a matter of hours. This means that you effectively maximize your potential audience and become visible to a global market.

The key with any marketing campaign is to understand your audience and target your potential clients by giving them what they want. With viral marketing and link bait it is essential that you explore your market avenues before you begin spreading the word. This means that you are targeting the right audiences. It is all very well to reach a thousand new people in a day but what is the point if only a few of them have any interest or need for what you are doing.

Basic Viral Marketing Tips

- Define your market

Before you plunge headfirst into a viral campaign you need to understand your market. This simply means that you will be able to target actual potential conversions. Ensure your campaign is geared towards viable audiences that will convert to customers.

- Bait and wait

A good hook is essential for viral marketing. Link bait is the key to increasing links and in turn maximizing your traffic. Good content is the best form of link bait.

- Get people talking

A little bit of controversy is great for viral marketing. If you can create a stir in your industry back links will be the result. It's a great way to reach a lot of people and grab some attention.

- Explore your avenues

How are the people in your industry communicating? What are they talking about? Blogs are great for viral marketing and getting your hook noticed. Look into forums, podcasting and other forms of communication being used in your industry. It's important to be active in your industry in order to create a strong visible brand.

Controversial Link Bait

One of the most interesting techniques to emerge in link baiting is that of the controversial hook. There are many forms of link bait that can effectively increase your link popularity. This kind of bait is perhaps one of the most talked about tricks of the trade. In fact that is the whole point. Controversy gets people talking, it generates interest, press and publicity in turn this is a great way to increase visibility and backlinks.

The modern link bait controversial comment is much like the traditional publicity stunt in a lot of ways. Posting something controversial, contrary or debatable can potentially generate thousands of quick links. Whether those links will convert into customers is another story all together but the point is traffic, backlinks and as a result increased rankings. This is all positive for your site but there are a few negative aspects of this kind of baiting.

The main thing to remember is with any kind of controversial link bait what you say or do reflects on your business. Using attack hooks or controversial comments to bait links is effective in a lot of ways but you need to consider carefully what your comments are saying about your business. There are lots of ways to get attention using a controversial hook so be creative rather than nasty and you will reap the benefits.

Try something like a controversial article about a mainstream corporation, idea, or individual. Create a controversial video, cartoon strip, anything that will grab attention for being "out-there"! N.B. People love stuff that is "out-there".

Benefits of controversial link bait.

- Instant traffic – If your post, comment or actions create a stir you will get an influx of traffic and backlinks. This is where your bait can have a viral effect. Once people are talking it is only a matter of time before they are linking.
- Link Popularity – Search engines dig sites with lots of back links. If you are creating a buzz in your industry and getting links from related sites then you have achieved success. The greater your link popularity the higher your ranking and this will hopefully lead to actual customers not just people that want to have a go.
- Visibility – They say no press is bad press so this kind of link bait can be good for business. The more people you get through the door the more exposure you are generating for your brand.
- Generate interest – You could potentially generate long-term interest if you engage in regular debate on hot topics or simply start a war of words with a well-known expert. This can create ongoing links and increase the opportunity for more backlinks.

Drawbacks of controversial link bait.

- Credibility – Your businesses credibility goes on the line every time you post something on your site or someone else's. There is a line and when using this kind of link bait you need to be aware of where that is. Make sure that controversy is not your only calling card. If people think that's all you're about your links won't last long.

- Overshadowing – Sometimes the controversy overshadows your actual brand or what you're trying to achieve. Again find the line and go to the edge but be careful not to create so much drama your message gets lost.
- Experts – One of the best kinds of backlinks you can get is one from a well-known expert. If you are stirring up your community by attacking experts or writing about industry leaders then you will loose out on valuable links in the future.

CHAPTER FOUR – LINK BAITING

Breaking Down Link Baiting

There is a lot of misconception about the concept of link baiting. Many people believe it is too complicated and time consuming for the average small business owner. The truth is anyone can succeed online; it may only take one piece of bait. Link baiting is easy because it's all about creating something unique to your site and business.

If you follow some basic general steps you can enhance your link popularity without too much trouble. Of course hiring a consultant is a great option but link baiting services are very costly and if you're an SME you need to properly work on a budget. The best way to get started is to gain some understanding as to how a campaign works and is broken down.

Firstly if you are going to manage your own campaign you will need to understand the concept. Link baiting is about sending out a hook so that people will link back to your site because they are compelled to do so by the quality or originality of the information. Your primary initiative is to establish whom you are trying to reach. Define your market. If you are going for industry specific traffic then you need to come up with a hook that will appeal to that audience. If you are aiming to appeal to a wider market and increase traffic in general then you have a little more room to move.

The hook should be something new, fresh and worthwhile. If you are aiming for a targeted audience you need to provide something useful, controversial or unique to your industry. For the more general audience you can go for something humorous and outrageous. Once you have decided on your angle, you then need to create the bait. This might be as simple as writing an article, adding a news section to your site or posting a comment on your blog or someone else's. The process can be a little more complicated than that however if you want to get technical. Some of the best forms of link bait are technical tools or gimmicks. These can be difficult to make if you do not have technical support. It is worth hiring a developer to do this for you, as you will see a good return on investment if your tool is useful to the industry or if it's amusing.

Once you have developed the bait, post it on your site and see what happens. You can monitor your link popularity using tools such as page rank, technorati or marketleap. It's a good idea to make it easy for people to bookmark your site or link to you. You can also request feedback and comments. If you have great bait the impact will be visible in a very short time span. If your bait is a flop then back to the drawing board. The trick is to keep at it. Every great idea is preceded by failures. That is how you learn what your market wants and what is best for your site. Link baiting is an ongoing process that when incorporated with sound marketing and SEO can turn your business around.

The art of link baiting comes down to consistency and perseverance. Be consistently providing useful information, news or content. Persevere with link baiting gimmicks and tricks. You never know one day you might just create the next subservient chicken or flying spaghetti monster.

Link baiting for SMEs

Perhaps those most significantly affected by the link baiting wave are that of small to medium sized enterprises. The Internet is home to millions of business, websites striving for visibility in a media frenzy. It can seem impossible to compete with all that is out there on the World Wide Web. The big guns have big budgets and premium exposure whereas SME's have to fight for the scraps.

The latest trends in Internet marketing may very well have evened out the playing field a little. Link baiting is a favorable option for turning around your business on the Internet. Anyone can be successful via a link baiting campaign. All it takes is a little time and perseverance. Creativity is key when it comes to putting your SME on the map.

Link baiting is all about creating something so useful people are drawn to it and are compelled to tell others about it by linking to you. Content is key for SME's. You don't have to have a huge budget to make great content that will be of use to your customers. If you can achieve this you are half way there when it comes to link baiting. The basic premise is to find a hook or an angle that will attract the right kinds of links and the right kind of visitors.

For an SME market research is imperative. Explore your community both online and in reality. Ideally you want to become a leader in your community. You are not trying to compete with the world you are simply trying to present yourself as a leader in your world. This is the easy part. Presenting your business as a leading resource will generate interest. The trick is doing this consistently and ensuring that when your visitors log on they are getting what they want.

Load your site with quality relevant content that will inform and educate your audiences as well as entertaining them. Become a resource for all things industry related. Get your name out there in the community using press releases, blogs, forums and podcasts. Trade links with related and complementary sites. Host experts on your site, their writing, resources, interviews, and reviews.

Optimize your site for search engine success. Generally if the search engine approves you can be sure the visitors will too. These days search engines are smart and you should perform to their criteria as much as you can. The number one factor in rankings is good content. This is a great place to start your link baiting campaign.

SME's rely on the quality of the product or service and the credibility of the brand. Creating brand awareness online can be difficult when you are a SME. That is why link baiting is so important. The more links you generate the greater your visibility becomes on the Internet. Visibility is essential if you are going to succeed.

Link baiting can enhance your businesses visibility in a number of ways. A lot of the techniques generate buzz, hype or interest. Link baiting is great for optimizing search engine rankings. Link baiting begins with good content, which is great for business any way you look at it.

On a meta-level, linkbait is something interesting enough to catch people's attention. While the term now carries some negative connotations, the negative elements are essentially a misnomer. Linkbaiting is not designed to be a bad thing. There are a lot of ways to do it and they include the noble but time-consuming efforts to generate data or insights organically; that is, by being creative. You can also think up something controversial to generate discussion. Provide a how-to video about a product you sell. The list goes on. Here are some examples.

Example 1: One blogger sat down and checked the spam filtering accuracy of SpamCop, Yahoo Mail, and Gmail to generate interesting content for his blog. Putting in the work generated insights on the differences between the competing services and certainly produced the type of info-laden content that makes a site or blog well-known over time.

Example 2: Look up the person, Marc Hil Macalua, who created a means of voting on head-to-head battles between SEOs. This didn't require a great deal of work; it required creative insight and a little work. Figure out how to grab people's attention and generate discussion.

Example 3: Saying something controversial definitely works. Look to Threadwatch and GoogleWatch for more information on this one. You can also look up the likes of Andrew Orlowski, who generated a lot of traffic by taking potshots at Google or blogs was a way to generate lots of discussion. Be careful, though. This linking niche gets worn out fast.

Example 4: Back to something creative: the *Google: Evil or Not?* site. It allows RSS feeds that mention Google, lets people vote between Real Good or Real Evil, and adds a graph. It took a little bit of work but it wasn't too expensive to pull together.

Overall, linkbaiting sometimes like a negative, underhand thing. However, if the content is interesting or funny, it is a great way to generate attention for your site. I hereby claim that content can be both white-hat and yet still be wonderful "bait" for links (e.g. Danny's spam email analysis). And generating information or ideas that people talk about is a surefire way to generate lin ks. Personally, I'd lean toward producing interesting data or having a creative idea rather than spouting really controversial ideas 100% of the time. If everything you ever say is controversial, it can be entertaining, but it's harder to maintain credibility over the long haul.

The future of linkbaiting really lies with great content. Search engines are going to distinguish between organic and inorganic content. The better your online content, the better your linking and the higher your rating.

Advantages for SME's

Link baiting is advantageous for a number of reasons for both your business and your customers. The process of linking baiting is in its most simplified form is about making your site more useful. Link baiting is about providing something of worth so that people will naturally want to link to you.

The advantages of this for your customers are that they have access to valuable information, tools, resources, downloads etc. The advantages for your business are more substantial.

- Free links

If someone naturally links to your site that means you have a free link. These are useful for a number of reasons. Primarily click through links generate a lot of traffic and if you have a number of sites linking to you then you are going to generate a lot of free links. Incoming links are also great for search engine rankings.

- Increased Traffic

One of the most significant advantages of link baiting is that of increased traffic. Link baiting produces two forms of traffic. The first is the click through link; this is helpful for increasing short-term traffic. Secondly link baiting will inevitably increase your search engine ranking which will increase your long-term traffic.

- Site promotion

Link baiting in its various forms gets your site noticed. Whether you are creating a controversy, providing expert advice or tools your site is being promoted. Link baiting is a popular way to market your site and to get people talking about your business.

- Increased search engine ranking

Search engines look at link popularity when ranking web pages. If you have a high number of incoming links then your site will rank higher in the results. This is because sites that have a lot of incoming links are generally considered useful and relevant. If other sites are linking to you then there is a good chance the search engine will consider your site to be important. An increased search engine ranking can be great for business. It could potentially turn your company around.

The Advantages of Link Baiting - Users

Link baiting is all about generating links in order to get visitors through the door in the hope that they will link to you. Link baiting is also very useful for boosting search engine rankings. These two factors have serious implications for business. The more traffic you get the more likely you are to be increasing your business potential and maximizing profits. As your traffic grows as a result of link baiting so does the value of your product or service. The more traffic you have coming in, the more links you will be making and so the cycle goes. Incoming links are great for search engine rankings too so once you get the ball rolling you are on the fast track to success.

All this is great for business but what about the customers? The fortunate thing about link baiting is that the majority of its techniques actually benefit the customer. The basic idea of link baiting is to create content so useful that people can not resist linking to it. Link baiting in this way creates natural links.

So when you embark on a link baiting campaign the aim is to refine your sites content to make it stronger and more useful for your customers. This is great all round. There are a number of benefits for your visitors that will also benefit your traffic and ranking.

- Site content

Normally link baiting will see an increase in site content. This content is not going to be search engine fodder but healthy relevant content that will provide benefits to customers. Building useful content is one of the best ways to keep your visitors coming back and to encourage them to link to your site.

- Updates

Webmasters often bait links by posting regular news updates, reviews and buzz pieces. These kinds of posts can generate a lot of links whilst also being very useful and entertaining for visitors. If you can provide industry relevant information on a regular basis essentially the site will become a one stop shop for people in your field.

- Reciprocal linking

This is another great way to maximize your link popularity and give your visitors what they want. Reciprocal links provide an avenue for your visitors to link to credible, related or complementary sites via your site. This means that you are providing expert links. This is just another way you are helping your visitors find what they are looking for.

- Tools

Link bait also comes in the form of useful tools or resources. These provide customers with the latest tools and resources for their everyday use. A good tool, calculator or resource can greatly enhance your link popularity and at the same time give your visitors something to talk about.

Myths

The idea of link baiting has exploded rapidly on the Internet. Like most Internet phenomenon this one has spread like a virus across the virtual super highway. Everywhere you turn people are talking about link baiting. As with lots of information you find online some of it is good while some is just plain myth.

So how do you determine between fact and fiction when it comes to link baiting? It is not so much a matter of right and wrong it is more about finding out what works and what is going to hinder you more than it helps.

There are a number of myths floating around about link baiting:

- All links are good links.

This is a myth. Not all links will help your site gain valuable rankings. If you have a lot of links coming in from unrelated, unknown sites the search engine will overlook your link popularity. The idea is quality not quantity. Links from related pages and well-known sites are best for improving your ranking and getting the right kind of people through the virtual door.

- Link baiting guarantees results

This is a popular myth that needs to be dispelled. Link baiting is not a surefire technique in fact it takes time and knowledge to perfect a campaign. Even then there are no guarantees your campaign will generate the results you desire. The problem is that too many people are looking for a quick fix. With link baiting the process is ongoing. If you plan to make the most out of your incoming links then you need to be providing new information on a regular basis. The purpose of these links is to generate more links so you need to constantly be giving them something to talk about.

- Controversy is key

Controversy is great for stirring up some interest but it's only a short-term solution. Initially this is a good way to get a lot of links coming in but without proper back up this technique will not do you justice. If you are going to focus on stirring up the industry as a major part of your link baiting campaign then be prepared to keep the controversy coming. People will quickly tire of rehashed ideas and controversy for the sake of controversy.

- Quantity is better than quality

Some people think that creating a whole lot of useless content will help to boost their rankings. In fact it will do the opposite. Search engines are wise to these techniques and users certainly have never appreciated search engine fodder. Quality content is the key to link baiting success. It is better to have one great article than ten that don't make sense. Link baiting is about attracting people and holding their attention. Quality rules over quantity from whatever angle you are coming from.

Linking Dos and Don'ts

- **Do link to pages of relevance that complement your site and your visitors' needs.**

- Don't submit your site to hundreds of paid directories, they do not return traffic and they are costly and ineffective.

- **Do create a list of relevant gurus or experts in your field, if this takes off and reaches the right people you could get some great expert links.**

- Don't spam other people's blogs, if you are going to post to plug your site do so in amongst useful comments.

- **Do review popular products on your site. Reviews are great for attracting traffic and links. If you keep updated and regularly review products you will maintain good rates of traffic.**

- Don't send automated pings to blogs or forums. If you are going to post ensure your comments are relevant and personalized. Don't post the same comments on a lot of sites.

- **Do get involved with relevant discussions and network within your community. This is a great way to expand your network and create linking opportunities.**

- Don't send automated emails to other webmasters requesting link trades. This is a surefire way to get your site black listed. If you are going to try the reciprocal linking route then personalize your requests.

- **Do consider hiring a consultant to help you with link baiting. An expert consultation can be effective in identifying where you can attract the most links. Once you have an idea about the best avenues to target you are halfway there.**

- Don't submit your links or site to pages that host hundreds of other links. Your link will get lost and be effectively redundant.

- **Do use your personal connections to create linking opportunities. Places like conferences, social events and business events are a great place to make connections. Establish relationships that could potential translate in to online links.**

- Don't covert content written by well-known web authors just to attract attention to your site.

- **Do be patient when attempting to bait links. You may not get an overwhelming response to begin with but if you continue with good link baiting practices you will see success.**

- Don't bombard webmasters with emails, referrals of false promises. This is not a good way to get traffic to your site.

- Do look into the possibility of becoming a sponsor or get involved with a charity. This is a good way to generate interest in your site.

- Don't attract bad press just for the sake of link baiting. It's one thing to post a controversial comment but its another thing entirely to sue your grandmother just to get links.

- Do ensure your site is clean, professional and up to date. There is no quicker way to turn your bait into hate than a sloppy website; broken links or heavy download times. Do the basics well and you will see results.

- Don't overload your site with poor quality content just to entice the search engines. Quality is key and search engines are smart. Good content that is of use to your visitors is fundamental to link baiting success.

- Do be creative. When it comes to link baiting your idea could be the next big thing on the net. The face of Internet marketing changes every day. Put your ideas into practice and create something new. The best way to beat the competition is not by being like them, it's by being unique.

- Don't waste your time with quick fix schemes and black hat scams. Integrity goes a long way and your credibility is your bread and butter online.

- Do create something funny, interesting, useful or cool on your site. The best type of gimmick is an interactive one.

- Don't be afraid to be different. If your idea is a flop then it will be forgotten about in seconds but if it's a hit you could be saturated with incoming links.

Common errors

The most common errors people make in link baiting are the same ones being made across the board when it comes to Internet marketing. When are people going to learn that less is more and quality rules over quantity? In recent years there has been an exponential surge in Internet marketing techniques. Everyday new avenues to plug your site and business are being uncovered. So why not just jump on the bandwagon and ride the wave of Internet hysteria all the way to the bank?

The answer is that while some of these more black hat techniques may bring you short-term success the ramifications will far out last the profits. The most common error people make in link baiting is to follow the crowd. When you jump on board with new techniques you need to consider what the outcomes may be for your business and its credibility.

Type in the keywords link baiting into any search engine, look at the results. This new push for link popularity is exploding as we speak. It is tempting to dive head first into a link baiting campaign without a second thought. The truth is that rushing into something like link baiting is a big mistake. Like any other marketing ploy before you begin marketing you need to understand the market. It's the same with link baiting. You need to know what your potential customers or clients are looking for. What kind of content would be useful for them? What kinds of tools would create a buzz? What are people within your industry talking about? Before you can even begin link baiting you need to ask yourself those questions and a whole lot more?

Another common error in link baiting is to overdo it. Link baiting is primarily a natural way to get people to link to your site. Sure the techniques are purposeful and targeted but you're not trying to force anyone into linking to you. People will link to you because they think you have worthwhile content. Many webmasters go down the path of automation. Whatever business you are in and whatever you are trying to sell automated emails, postings and comments are a huge mistake. If you are trying to trade links, generate interest, or create some buzz about your business the personal approach is best. Use automated site scanners so that you can identity possible targets but appeal to them on a personal level.

When you are trying to market something you need to have an understanding of what it is you are offering to your customers. Do not make the mistake of singular or one way marketing. When it comes to link baiting you should not just go all out with your plug. Remember you are trying to get people to link to you because they want to. If you present as only caring about what they can do for you then you will fail before you begin. Create relevant content, discuss topical information and invite people to spread the buzz. The same applies when posting on forums or blogs or when sending referral emails. Point out what the benefits are for the potential visitor or customer before you start to plug your site.

One of the most prominent and damaging mistakes webmasters make is trying to trick the search engines. Search engines access link popularity when ranking pages. Many webmasters believe that the quality and relevance of the links is not important. The opposite is in fact true. Most search engines will overlook links to sites that are unrelated or not credible. This could damage your ranking and in turn hinder your opportunity for more links.

Finally the biggest mistake you can make is not considering link baiting in your marketing campaign. Link baiting can take your business to the next level and turnaround your development. For SME's link baiting can be the turnaround factor. If you don't try then you will never know how high your ranking could go or how much you could improve your business. Visibility and exposure are key to a successful web presence. Without those two factors your business will be virtually invisible. A good link baiting campaign can increase your page views like you never imagined.

Short term link bait

Ideally when designing link bait you want to look for something that is going to return long term results for your site. The best links are those that will give you a steady stream of traffic for a longer period of time. In your ranking, search engines will consider the strength and endurance of your links. Search engines consider strong links to be those that come from related credible sites. These are the sorts of links you should be targeting.

Short-term link bait can be great for your immediate traffic and for your ranking. There are lots of ways to create link bait that will have a viral effect. A sudden influx of traffic usually means your link is being passed on. Potentially you can reach a hugh number of people in a short amount of time simply by creating a good hook.

Here are some great ways to stir up immediate interest for short-term links.

- Create a controversy

Controversy is a sure-fire way to get a big hit of traffic and an influx of incoming links. There are many ways you can put your site on the map with a good scandal. With this kind of link bait you can attract both positive and negative attention. Positive attention comes from the search engines whereas some publishers may not appreciate the bait. The most common form of controversial link bait is that of an attack hook. This entails making a dig at someone well known in the industry, a webmaster, blogger or expert. This can get an instant response and is a good way to drum up some quick links.

- Run a contest

Contests are good for creating a buzz about your site and procuring incoming links. It doesn't have to be something extravagant or costly, simply creative and eye catching. A good contest can generate a healthy amount of backlinks in a short amount of time. This is a great short-term solution.

- Invite a guest

One way to create some quick links is to have a guest post on your site or blog. Get someone interesting, an expert or well-known figure to appear on your site. People will be lining up to link to this kind of bait. This is an effective way to get a lot of people visiting your site and linking the information. You can also achieve this by posting interviews of interest on your site or blog.

- Giveaways, freebies and free trails

People love free stuff. Giveaways stir up interest in your site, generate links and have a viral effect. People will tell their friends if it is something worthwhile. This will increase your short-term traffic and help you promote your product or service.

Long term link baiting

Many strategies can increase your link popularity in the short term, ideally however those that have a long-term impact are better for business. Certain link baiting techniques can return a high number of links in a small amount of time but will not have a lasting effect on your link popularity. The best type of link bait is that which helps to increase your ranking and long-term prospects.

Examples of short-term link bait include bait such as a controversial or contrary hook. Other short-term link bait strategies are things like contests, awards, guest speakers, giveaways and press releases. These strategies can be great for creating a stream of incoming links on a short-term basis but they will not stand alone in creating ongoing popularity. Short term strategies will give your site an influx of visitors but in order to turn them into long term users you need to have something to back the bait up.

There is no substitute for good quality content as link bait. This may be the oldest technique in the book but it is certainly one of the best. Good content that is of use to your visitors is great for long term results. Firstly useful content will be distributed via linking by your users to others. The more people you get to your site the more links you will generate. Audience focussed content is also appealing to search engines and will increase your ranking. A high search engine ranking is perhaps the most important thing for long term traffic. Good content equals links and good ratings which all add up to a high ranking.

Gimmicks are great and games are good for grabbing attention but they will not be as effective as other forms of bait. One of the gimmicks will get people through the door for a time but you need to offer something else as well. News is a good hook for long term bait. If you have a daily news section on your site you will get people coming back to it everyday and linking to it on their site or blog. News is a sure-fire way to get attention and keep it. Ideally focus on industry related stories that will spread like wildfire around your community. Be the first to post a story and you will increase your ranking significantly.

Promoting your site as useful and worthwhile is the best way to establish yourself as a leader in the industry. Provide the latest product or service reviews for your community. Reviews are a great way to establish a lot of backlinks. People value expert opinions and feedback and see reviews as a worthwhile resource.

Another great way to establish long-term links is by creating a meme or tool. Memes are something cute, useful, or gimmicky that others can put on their site but that links back to yourself. Examples of this are buttons, navigation systems, page layouts, avatars or tools. A useful tool hosted on your site is also a good way to attract backlinks.

Link baiting was propelled into mainstream media when it became a hot topic in the SEO blog community. In fact blogs are actually great link bait and they are great for spreading link bait too. A blog is an ongoing effort but the long-term effects are significant. Link baiting is a common trend in the blogosphere so the chances are connected to your community you will get a lot of long term backlinks. In the blogosphere permalinks are long term links that connect blogs across the network. Even when the post is removed from the front page the link remains intact so that people can view the page at any time. Blogs posts and comments are great link bait simply due to the interconnectedness of the blogosphere.

CHAPTER FIVE – BUDGETS

Link baiting on a budget

Link bait is the new buzzword in Internet marketing. The concept, which has been around for years, is now one which serious Internet and SEO marketers are integrating into their campaigns. Link baiting is about appealing to users and search engines by providing content that is so useful people are inclined to link to it. Nowadays link popularity is of such importance that the search engines consider page popularity a major factor when ranking that page.

So how do you compete with the big guns when you're a small to medium sized enterprise on a tight budget? The great thing about the Internet is that innovation and creativity count for a lot. For one thing, it's really easy to generate popularity and presence online by doing something relatively simple. Start a blog or start posting videos online at YouTube, Google Video, or MySpace. Create social profiles on sites like MySpace and Friendster and you can send links to your website at the touch of a button to anyone in your network of contacts or your extended network (people who know your friends). You can manage a successful link campaign with a very little budget that will return your investment and turn your business around.

The fundamental idea when it comes to link baiting is that if you have a quality site with useful and compelling information you already have a site prime for baiting links. It is true; great content is paramount to a successful link baiting campaign. If your site is already packed with good content then your job is a lot easier. If you lack a little in the content department, not to worry. Link baiting is easy to master and all it takes is a little knowledge and innovation.

Link baiting on a budget begins firstly by accessing what you already have. What content is currently up on your site? Is there room for improvement in terms of quality? What is your brand position?

One of the most cost-effective ways to generate links is to improve the content on your site. Quality is better than quantity so your aim should be to have a good amount of top quality content. Articles are a great way to begin and can cost you very little. Start with developing news articles, resource articles or lists. These are simple yet very effective for link baiting. If you can't write the articles yourself then you can hire a writer for a relatively nominal fee.

Post the articles on your site and submit them to free directories. If you can find some relevant sites in your industry that host articles free, post them there. Also you can host articles on your site in exchange for links.

Another way to attract links as well as search engine rankings is to clean up your site. You can do this yourself without spending a cent. Make sure your keywords are working for you. Do some market research to really define your audiences. Clean design, simple layouts and a small amount of page content is best for SEO purposes.

Blogs are simple, to manage and cost effective for those on a limited budget. Start up a blog and get interactive with your community. Post regularly, post creatively and keep your audience updated. Blogs are ideal for generating click through links and for increasing your link popularity. Also you can always post on other peoples blogs free. You can become an active expert in your industry, create a controversy or simply network for connections.

Get people talking, if you can get people discussing your site and its content your link popularity will improve. Submit regular press releases within the industry to drum up interest and inform your users of updates. Hire a writer to construct a newsletter that you can distribute free to customers or potential industry contemporaries.

Post news on your site. The best kind is industry specific, as this will give your customers a reason to keep coming back. If you can keep up with the latest news and get it up on your site first you will increase your link popularity significantly.

Review new products, or old products that are newsworthy. Review sites and blogs on your site. This is easy enough to do and won't cost you a thing. Just make sure you are accurate and precise when reviewing technical products.

Run a small contest. You can offer small cash prizes or giveaway product or services. Contests are good for getting people to visit your site. This means that you have an opportunity to hook them with your content. Once someone is hooked you will find they are inclined to link to you and to talk about your site.

Run a poll about something topical. Ask visitors to vote and then acquire their email address so you can send them the results. The more you get people interacting on your site the more links you will get coming in.

The one thing you need to remember when it comes to link baiting is that creativity is the key to success. You don't have to have a big budget to fully capitalize on the link-baiting phenomenon. Many small to medium sized enterprises fail to reach their potential simply because they are unable to translate their skills and knowledge into a successful Internet marketing strategy. The beauty of link baiting is that you might already be doing it simply by having a site with great content.

For businesses that are struggling with the concept you don't need to look far to discover the latest techniques, tips and tricks in the book. Spend some time reading about the concepts, ideas and techniques that are turning businesses around. The most powerful tool you have is knowledge, therefore increase yours and watch the links roll in.

Money to burn

For companies with a big budget link baiting can literally take your business to the next level. If you have money to burn you have a number of high tech options that could potentially see your site in the top ten. This is the aim of a link baiting campaign. Creating a site that is optimal for both users and search engines is no easy task and it can be a very time consuming process. For those on a big budget there are a few significant options.

Firstly you may consider hiring a link baiting, SEO or marketing specialist. These gurus are experts in the field of Internet marketing and all its intricate ins and outs. Link baiting specialists have emerged in recent months equipped to handle extensive baiting campaigns. A specialist is ideal for big budget clients as they will handle the whole process and you are almost certainly guaranteed results. A consultant of this nature will work to build your sites content, identify target markets and avenues for link bait as well as manage the implementation and monitoring of the campaign.

Another great way to generate a large amount of links if you have the money is to hire a developer. A good developer can create useful tools, games, and interactive media that can all be placed on your site to increase link popularity. These sorts of resources can have a huge impact on your link popularity and have the potential to explode onto the rankings. A useful way to increase your links is to have a collection of tools that your visitors can use and link to.

Content is key for link baiting purposes. Good content is a great hook and can see your link popularity skyrocket. Hire an excellent web writer who is well-versed in SEO content writing. You can have a writer produce regular articles, newsletters, daily buzz pieces, in depth features, resources lists, blog entries etc. If you can consistently be producing useful content and news on a daily basis your link popularity will be unstoppable. If you find the right writer you can have them manage the entire content campaign so all you have to do is sit back and watch the links roll in.

It is often useful to submit your site to paid directories in order to increase your rankings and exposure. If you have a big budget submitting to a number of credible paid directories could be of benefit. This is something that can enhance your sites visibility but beware the directories that just add your link to a page of thousands. Industry related directories are great as well as well-known general ones.

Expert opinions, pieces and appearances are great for credibility and therefore link popularity. If you can purchase the services of a well-known expert you will generate a lot of interest. Some possible options include an expert feature writer, podcast host or guest forum speaker.

Basically if you have money to burn in the marketing department you have a world of options at your fingertips. However money as they say can't buy you love and if you can't back up your campaign with a quality product or service then your success will be short lived.

CHAPTER SIX – LINK BAITING IDEAS

The Hook

It is not always easy trying to get others to link to your site or blog. Often you have to look past simply trying to sell your product or service. You need something to draw people in; you need to find a way to get them to the door and through the door. Getting people to your door is something that can be achieved by successful link baiting. Link baiting is all about sending out a hook in order to get people to link to you naturally. Once you have people linking to you it has a sort of chain reaction. Links lead to more links and to link popularity, which leads to an increased search engine ranking. These are all bonuses for business.

Link bait is designed to attract attention in the hope that it will convert into valuable links. Link bait is the hook that will pull your customers in and get the wheels turning. So how do you hook people in? Crafting a hook is basic marketing common sense. You either have to get people talking or give them something to talk about. The possibilities are as limitless as your imagination when it comes to creating a viable hook.

Here are a few of the latest in link bait hooks:

Resource Hook

The resource hook is great for generating incoming links. People link to sites they find useful. Resources provide an excellent service to users, this will help establish your site as relevant and worthwhile and in turn increase your link popularity.

- Try hooking your users with a great new tool on your site. You can be creative with web tools by creating something purposeful or something fun related to your industry.
- Resource lists populated with outgoing links are a great way to hook other webmasters. You would be surprised at how many outgoing links translate into incoming ones. You can list links to blogs, useful websites, experts or gurus and more.
- Host advice or information articles on your site.
- Craft a 'how to' article or a 'top ten' article
- Provide a review page, analyze new products.
- Create a news section for relevant industry news

Aggressive Hook

This kind of hook is considered questionable by some webmasters. The truth is people love a good argument and controversy is a big seller. The aggressive hook involves verbally attacking someone else in order to generate interest and get people linking back to your site. While it can be a great way to get people talking it can also back fire so you need to choose your target and your words carefully.

- Post a comment on someone else's blog attacking their viewpoint or position on an industry-related topic.
- Post something nasty about a well-known expert or guru.

Contradictory Hook

This is the tamer version of the attack hook. Here you are trying to stimulate interactive debate and therefore drive traffic to your site. This is great for getting people interested and maintaining incoming traffic.

- Take an opposing view to everyone else in your community or industry about a new product or story.
- Post comments on why you disagree with everyone else.
- Purposefully disagree with a well-known expert
- Engage in blog debates and forum discussions.
- Write articles that disprove or question well-known and accepted theories.

Buzz Hook

News can be great link bait because if you can beat out the competition and get your story posted early your sites ranking will be significantly boosted. Once your site is up on the rankings the visitors will flock to your site for the inside scoop. This creates a good environment for linking.

- Have a news section on your site that you update everyday.
- Keep an archive of news.
- Create a newsletter
- Be the first to scoop a story.

Humor Hook

Laughter is the best medicine as they say; it's also a great hook. The humor hook has proven to be very effective on the Internet. Imagination and creativity are key for this kind of hook. If you can come up with something good not only will you get a few laughs you will generate link traffic.

- Create a funny interactive tool.
- Post a humorous photo of your product or something industry related.
- Post a funny list or article.

Top Ten Baiting Picks

Link baiting is a concept that is in constant motion. Every time you log on you will find new ideas; tricks and techniques designed to increase incoming links. Link popularity is a primary indicator of the relevance and importance of the information within a page. A high level of link popularity indicates to the search engine that the page should be well ranked. This is the aim of any person who embarks on a deliberate link baiting campaign. Out of all the tricks of the trade we have identified the top ten link baiting picks to boost your ranking and generate incoming links.

1. Create top ten articles

These are simple to create and easy to link to. You can create one that is relevant to your industry or try something fun, newsworthy or unique. You can experiment with top ten tip articles, lists, myths or downloads.

2. Lists

Construct a 101 ways list, these are similarly easy to link to and people get caught up in the craze. These lists if good can become great resources, as they are so easy to follow and can be helpful for experts as well as beginners. Experiment with what's hot and what's not lists.

3. Expert advice

Position yourself as an expert in your field through good quality content. You can use articles to bait links in so many ways and it is invaluable to your campaign. Submit articles to directories, have other experts link to your site by hosting articles on your site. Ensure your articles are of high quality and will be useful to others in your industry. Good content can help turn your company around.

4. Blog

Create a blog and stir up some interests. Blogs are a great way to get people interacting with you and in this way you can steer them towards linking to your site. Post comments on other blogs, you can be controversial if need be anything to get people clicking through.

5. Forum

Host a forum on your site. This is a great way to stir up interest, promote interactivity and bait links. Once you get a forum going you will have regular visitors that will lead to links. Keep your forum interesting, up to date and explore the latest relevant topics.

6. Directories

This is a tried and true method for increasing yours sites exposure. Submit your site to relevant directories. Free site submissions are a cost-effective way to drive traffic to your site. The more traffic you get the more chances you have for linking. When submitting your site to free directories stick to those that are credible such as DMOZ. You can also pay for submissions, always keep in mind quality over quantity.

7. Hold a contest

This is a great way to get people to your site and to bait links. You don't have to offer thousands of dollars in prizes to see a substantial return. Small contests can generate hundreds of viable links.

8. Create a Controversy

This is an interesting and creative way to get people to link to your site. You can do this in a number of ways. Comment on a well-known blog with an outrageous opposing view. Post something controversial on your site; post on someone else's forum or start a controversial blog. This is prime opportunity to get your creative juices flowing. If you can elicit a reaction out of people that gets them to your site then you are lining up the links.

9. Link Trading

Reciprocal links can be very useful but you must handle them correctly. Discriminate between a good and a bad link. Don't link to everyone; don't link to anyone just because you can. Stick to related sites and complementary industries. Do not use automated emails to request links. If you can trade links with credible contemporaries and well-known websites your links will go a lot further.

10. Tools

This has proven to be a highly effective form of link baiting. Create a useful tool or a collection of tools that will serve a purpose for your visitors. If you can create something of worth then you will have hooked yourself a linking gold mine.

Link baiting ideas

You don't need to be technologically advanced or a marketing guru to create good productive link bait. If you have a brand, something to sell or a service to provide then you can enhance your link popularity through link baiting. You see essentially link baiting is about sharing something useful with your audience. It's about encouraging interactivity online. Whether that be via discussion, controversy or content, link baiting promotes connections.

Coming up with a link baiting idea is easy if you know what you're doing. The key is in knowing what your audience is talking about and what they want to talk about. The first step is creating something that people will respond to. Once you have explored your market you will know what it is that your audience is interested in.

Whatever form your bait takes remember that the most important thing is being able to elicit a response. Many webmasters make the mistake of rehashing old ideas. Link bait should be new, interesting and exciting. It should make people want to learn more about your site or your content. Either way it should get them to link to you because what you have to say is important or news worthy.

There are hundreds of avenues for creating link bait. Over the next chapter you will be presented with a wealth of ideas to get you started when it comes to your own campaign.

Articles

Articles are a great way to build content on your site or to generate visibility on other sites. Informative well written articles can do a lot for building link popularity. Articles give you multiple opportunity to link during the content. These are the best kinds of links. Links embedded within the content of an article will considerably increase click through page views. The more page views you get the more links you generate.

- Write a specific top ten article. A top ten article on a subject related to your industry is a great way to get people to link to you e.g. top ten fad diets, top ten inspirational quotes, top ten recruitment agencies, top ten NLP techniques, top ten employee incentive programs. Of course the kind of article you write will depend on the industry you are in. These kinds of articles often become valuable resources. Top ten articles are very easy to link to.

- Write a general top ten article. Write an article on the 'top internet marketing tips, top ten SEO tricks, top ten link baiting tips, top ten design tips, top ten content tips, top ten internet scams, top ten reasons to link bait' etc. This is the time to get creative you can write about anything that you think will interest your visitors.

- Write an interesting article about something new in your industry. If you can be one of the first to write about it you will instantly boost your ranking and your link popularity. This kind of article is great for building link popularity as you will get attention from people within your field and these links are priceless.

- Write an article about something controversial. You can stick to your own field with this kind of article or branch out to something more general. Either way the aim is to get a response. A response may very well result in incoming links. If you can write something controversial about a newsworthy current subject then you are sure to get people fired up.

- Write an article about a well-known person and post it on your site.

- Write something funny. An article or anecdote with a touch of humor will entice people to link to your site.

- Write about a universal topic like religion with an outrageous opposing viewpoint. The Flying Spaghetti Monster or the Evangelical Scientist gravity theory are good examples of this type of link bait.

Tools

Using tools or gadgets to bait links has proven very effective. If you can come up with something creative, new and relevant to your visitors you will be fending off the links. These tools should be something people find useful enough to link to.

- Try developing some sort of calculator. This is interactive and can be very useful. Examples of these include; BMI indicator, currency converter, mortgage calculator, calorie counter, exercise prescription index, translator, budget calculator.

- Build a collection of useful tools that your visitors can link to. These can be related to your business or general in nature.

- Build to gimmick type tool that advertises your product. You can have a bit of fun with this whilst also promoting your product.

Contests

Contests are a great way to generate some interest in your site. They are time and cost effective and can generate a huge return. You can again be creative when coming up with ideas for contests. You don't have to spend a fortune on prizes to maximize the impact of this type of baiting. A few hundred dollars could very well translate into quality invaluable links.

- A simple article submission contest can expand your network as well generate links and rankings.

- Giveaways are always a good idea. Give away space on your site for hosting articles, offer link opportunities, and give away free consultations, samples or product testers in exchange for links, referrals or feedback.

- Run a contest for people to come up with the best link baiting idea.

- Run a contest that asks people to submit their blog for a best blog award.

- Run a contest for the best top ten lists.

Quizzes

Everyone loves a good quiz, whether it's a romance compatibility quiz or a mesa IQ test. These are great interactive ways to get people visiting your site and linking back to it. You can develop your quizzes to suit your industry or you can take a more general fun approach.

- Surveys, quizzes and tests are great because they get people interacting and connecting to your site. You can expand on this by offering regular quizzes that you can distribute by emails.

- Try a fun quiz as a gimmick, such as a relationship test or a style quiz.

- Get to know your visitors with an online survey.

- Offer serious tests like working style, personality classifications, marketing knowledge or job satisfaction tests.

News

One of the most effective ways to up your ranking and to get people to your site is to post news pieces. If you can be one of the first to post information about breaking news your site ranking will automatically be boosted.

- Create a buzz section on your site where you can post the latest news and updates.

- Become an authority in your field by keeping up to date with all the breaking news that affects you and your customers.

- Write expert news articles to host on your site and to submit to other sites.

- Submit news pieces to well known hosts such as GoArticles or Ezinearticles. These hosts have well ranked pages that will benefit your link popularity.

- Link with sites that have news sections.

- Submit press releases to inform interested parties when you are presenting new features, news or content.

- Start a news blog and kick it off with an attention grabbing story. Something that will get people talking is great, get them thinking and you will get them linking.

Lists

Lists are a great resource as they are simple, succinct and easy to follow. For the millions of web newbies lists are a godsend. Lists are also great link bait as they are easy to link to and are simple and cost effective to create. A list will promote you as an expert, provide valuable useful information to your customers and encourage people to link back to you.

- Create a 101 list. These are simple and effective. You can tailor them to suit any industry; any subject and they cost you nothing to create.

- Create a top ten list.

- Create a list of gurus or experts. These can be a great way to get these experts to link to your site. Credible links equals good rankings. These lists are also very useful for your visitors.

- Create a resource list for an industry specific subject. You can use this list to trade links as well as provide comprehensive information for your visitors.

- Create a resource list for a complementary industry. This is also a good way to trade links and you will be expanding your networks at the same time.

- Create a top ten common errors list.

- Create a list of favorite sites. Outgoing links are a good way to attract incoming ones.

- Create a list of useful articles.

- Create a list of useful blogs, this can be a great way to get bloggers to link to you. Target blogs that you would like a link from.

Blogging

Blogs are a highly interactive form of Internet communication. They are easy to manage and easy to link to making them ideal for building link popularity. Many webmasters are using blogs to reach a wider audience.

- Create your own blog, preferably one that is relevant to your site but if not you can always create a controversy.

- Post on other people's blogs. It is best not to go straight in for the kill when posting comments, save your plug till you are well established on the blog.

- Create a news blog. News is a great way to reach your audience, if you can post something new within your field the links will follow.

- Create a resource blog so that you can share your resources with your visitors and they can interact with you.

- List you blog in the top blog directories.

- Link to other blogs in your posts, outgoing links often generate incoming ones.

- Join the blogosphere. Blogs are community driven so create a community and increase your connections and your links.

Tips

Any content that might be useful to your visitors is considered link bait. Whether you are trying to attract links or not if you have useful tips, tricks of the trade, or advice you might be increasing your link popularity.

- Create a page for tips on your site. Become a resource site for your industry so that people have a reason to talk about your site.

- Create a page that other people can post tips on or comment on your tips. Get people interacting and the links will soon follow.

- Target people in your industry with helpful advice and useful tips and tricks. The more relevant to your industry your information is the more chance you will have of attracting people who can boost your link popularity through their sites.

- Be the first to come up with new tips and post them on your site. Anything new and fresh is optimal for boosting your link popularity.

- Create a page of links that offer your visitors useful tips and resources. This is great for your users as well as your link popularity.

- Post tips on other sites; position yourself as an expert.

Expertise

One of the best ways to gain credibility on the Internet is to position yourself as an expert. This will attract serious customers looking for good advice. There are a number of ways you can refine your site and your link baiting techniques to get the maximum effect.

- Write expert advice articles on subjects related to your industry.

- Create a resource for expert articles on your site.

- Create a list of other experts and gurus.

- Post articles on other peoples sites.

- Comment on well-known blogs and forums.

- Interview experts and post the interviews on your site.

- Have a writer do a feature on you that can be posted on news sites; related industry sites and blogs.

- When doing business request referrals from satisfied customers, friends or colleagues. These referrals can be sent out to potential clients.

- Request feedback from customers, testimonials and reviews.

- Review products and services related to your industry. Review other expert sites.

- Say something nice about an expert.

- Ask for feedback and reviews from experts and post them on your site.

Games

There is nothing like a little fun to get people in the mood to link. Interactive games are a great way to get people to link to your site. This kind of link baiting can be more costly but its potential is limitless if you can create something innovative and new.

- Create an interactive game that people can play on your site. It doesn't have to be Warcraft rather something simple and accessible that will entertain your visitors.

- Link to interactive gaming sites.

- Create a little test like hand coordination, reaction tester, or a brainteaser.

- Create something familiar like a small PAC man game or a block building game.

- Create a design game, where you can build something, design something or add your own flare to a static design.

- Build a game page with games that relate to your industry.

Create a controversy

This is an interesting and innovative way of generating page views and attracting business. Some of the methods have been extreme while others are tamer. The important thing to remember is that not all press is good press and the credibility of your business will be on the line every time. The fact is however controversy sells and if you can get people talking then the links will not be far behind the conversation.

- Post a controversial comment on some else blog. This is good if it's an industry blog with a lot of users.

- Post a controversy on your own blog or site.

- Sue Google, this has its drawbacks but has been done before and will create a lot of hype. Do so at your own risk however.

- Get sued.

- Post comments about a well known person

- Post industry secrets on your site.

- Write a controversial article and submit it to article directories.

- Criticize someone important in your industry. This will only work in the long term if you actually know what you are talking about.

Podcasts

Podcasting is great link bait. The key to an effective podcast is to update regularly and make it unique and useful.

- Create a postcast targeted at people within your industry. Information, tips and news will generate links.

- Create a controversial podcast that is either useful or entertaining. Make sure it's related to your product or service.

Interviews

Interviews are a great way to generate short-term links that could turn into long-term profits. Interviews can drum up attention, provide interesting information and give your site credibility.

- Interview a leading expert in your field and post it on your site.

- Interview your competitors and post it on your site.

- Interview useful experts in complementary fields.

- Interview someone in the current news headlines.

- Interview clients or customers for feedback purposes.

- Interview some on your podcast and transcribe the interview.

Awards

Awards generate a lot of interest and can be an effective way to attract linking opportunities. Awards should be relevant and meaningful in order to maximize their potential.

- Create an industry award with meaningful criteria and strict guidelines.

- Create a complementary industry award

- Create an award for your clients or customers.

- Create an expert award.

- Create a blog, forum or podcast award.

Videos

This is a fairly new concept for link baiting but one that is taking off with extraordinary pace. A useful video can be a gold mine for link baiting purposes. Fundamentally videos should be professionally created, informative and brief.

- Create an informative video.

- Create a funny video.

- Create an instructional video.

Special Guests

Inviting an expert or special guest to comment or interact on your site will generate a lot of interest and links. This is a great way to cross advertise, increase your link popularity and provide a great resource for your visitors.

- Invite a guest to appear on your podcast.

- Invite a guest to comment on your forum.

- Invite a guest to write for your blog.

- Invite an expert to exchange writing on your site.

- Invite an expert to appear on a live chat on your site.

Press releases

Press releases are a great social networking tool and provide an excellent angle for link baiting. Post them on blogs, forums, news sites and podcasts.

- Announce new products, services with a press release.

- Announce new features to your site with a press release.

- Announce guest speakers or experts that will be contributing to your site.

- Announce new or proposed resources on your site.

- Announce changes in the industry.

- Announce new tools, games, blogs, forums or upcoming podcasts.

Newsletters

Ezines and newsletters are ideal for generating ongoing traffic and creating multiple linking opportunities. This type of media should be informative, insightful and interesting. The aim is to keep people on the subscription list and for them to tell others about you.

- Have a weekly, fortnightly or monthly newsletter go out to all your current customers informing them of new offers, features, news etc.

- Send out an annual report with useful information about your industry.

- Give readers the option to tell a friend on the newsletter.

- Subscribe to industry related newsletters and make comment on them.

- Link to your site as much as possible during the newsletter.

- In your newsletter give a little snippet of information so that readers have to click through to your site for more information.

Directories

There are many credible well-known directories that allow you to submit your site or pages to their lists. This is great for increasing visibility and expanding your networks. A good directory listing means people that may not have been able to find you now have access to your site and information.

- Submit your site to free directories, stick to credible ones.

- Submit your site to paid directories; again don't pay for something that's not going to give you a good return. Select carefully.

- Submit articles you have written to articles directories

- Submit your blog to blog directories. This is a great way to attract links and there are many very credible blog channels.

Consultation

Hiring a professional is a very effective way to manage your link baiting campaign. There are many reputable companies and individuals now offering link baiting services. These are link-baiting experts that can help you develop link baiting techniques that are sure to get results.

- Hire a link baiting specialist

- Hire a SEO consultant

- Hire an internet marketing guru

- Hire a corporate turnaround firm

Memes

Meme's can be gimmicky or they can be very useful. Either way it is great link bait as people will be using them on their own sites. Meme's are little tools, buttons, and characterizations, navigation systems or menus that can be replicated and used on other sites with a backlink to the origin.

- Create a cute button meme

- Create a navigation system that others can use.

- Create a menu.

- Create an avatar that can be replicated

Tips and Tricks

- Tip – Create something useful that will increase brand visibility and enhance your brand positioning. Example Rand's <u>Page Strength Tool</u>.

- **Trick – Ask members of a forum to review your site and offer feedback. This will generate a lot of backlinks.**

- Tip – Create a separate page for awards, contests, games, reviews, interviews, links tools, social interests or anything else you think your visitors might be interested in. Example <u>Web 2.0</u> site by SEOmoz

- **Trick – Write something nice about sites you want to link to. This is a sneaky way of avoiding link requests and chances are if you write something good the webmaster will link to you.**

- Tip – Create an onsite directory where other sites in your industry can submit their links. This will set you up as a resource site for your visitors. Example <u>Search Engine Guide</u> for small businesses by Jennifer Laycock

- **Trick - If the nice approach fails, you can always try writing something nasty.**

- Tip – Create a cool brand specific gimmick, character, tool or interactive game. Example Burger Kings <u>Subservient Chicken</u>

- **Trick – Approach the owner or web master of a site you want to link to and ask for an interview. Post the interview on your site and the owner/webmaster is sure to link to it.**

- Tip – Start a blog community for industry specific news and views. Invite industry leaders, experts, and gurus who you would like to link to and post them invitations to become a blog publisher on your site. Example <u>Perfomancing.com</u> by Nick Wilson

- **Trick – Write an article with embedded links to your sites and submit it to article directories and site hosts.**

- Tip – Create a useful list with plenty of good ideas or resources. Link to other sites in the list. Example <u>101 ways to build link popularity</u> in 2006 by Aaron Wall and Andy Hagan

- **Trick – Write an article about link baiting it's a hot topic at the moment.**

- Tip – Challenge a well establish theory, person, system, structure. Example Church of the <u>Flying Spaghetti Monster</u>

- **Trick – Run a poll to see whom users vote the best site in your industry. The winner will be inclined to link to your site.**

CHAPTER SEVEN – THE GRAY AREA

Shades of gray

The general definition of link bait is 'something that causes others to back link to a site naturally.' Link baiting is considered a natural form of generating incoming links but certain practices within the link baiting definitions are not organic. The problem with generalized definitions is they come from a binary perspective, black or white, organic or inorganic. Link baiting requires further examination and perhaps dualistic definition.

The debate is over whether all link baiting can be considered natural, as there is a specific purpose to a link baiting campaign. There are also techniques widely considered link baiting techniques that go beyond natural linking. These include reciprocal linking, trading links and PPC advertising. Across the board many experts consider these to be within the realm of link baiting. Others believe that the basic notion of natural linking is true link baiting.

This basic notion specifies that true link bait is simply great content. That is content so useful, amusing or interesting webmasters and publishers will naturally link to it. Link baiting however has evolved into something that surpasses this simplistic definition. Link baiting is now an industry with purpose and direction that does often go beyond natural techniques.

This is the gray area of link baiting. How do you define what is natural and organic when most link baiting nowadays is part of a link popularity campaign. Does this mean that optimizing your sites content to increase links is no longer organic? How do we define what is truly natural linking when there link baiting is results driven and goal orientated.

The idea is that if a site is truly worthwhile and its content is constructed with audiences in mind then natural links are inevitable. Links acquired by not so natural means like trading still fall under the definition of link baiting as the site content must be appealing enough to attract the backlink. It is hard to categorically define such a broad and wide spread concept so it is best to just accept the gray.

Link bait is an all encompassing term that includes techniques that attract natural links and techniques that are not necessarily natural. Link baiting campaigns are now more than just creating good content and leaving the rest to chance. Link bait is deliberate and purposeful.

Other techniques that fall into the gray area include:

- Directory submissions
- Automated link requests
- Manual link requests

Organic Link Bait vs Inorganic Link Bait

When the term link bait first emerged in mainstream Internet marketing it was an organic concept. The definition included those practices that created natural linking. Since the term has exploded there has been extensive examination of the concepts included in its definition. Organic link bait is bait that attracts links naturally while non organic link bait is more targeted and purposeful but is still consider a natural form.

There are a few differences between organic link bait and inorganic methods. Firstly organic link bait is not purposeful designed link bait. It is more likely that this link bait comes in the form of content. Before the link bait push there was the usability explosion. Webmasters began looking at usability techniques in order to enhance user experiences. This often entailed upgrading sites to provide resources to users and refining content and site specifications to suit a target audience. These types of modifications can be considered link bait, but they are truly organic because they are not designed for getting links. These kinds of practices are created specifically for users and not as specialized link bait.

Organic link bait also includes other techniques generally used on a site that are not purposeful link bait. Some argue that nowadays everything a webmaster does to enhance their site is just link bait. Organic link baiting does include enhancement techniques as they allow for natural linking and are not asking for links or using deliberate provocation tricks.

Inorganic link baiting is not a bad thing at all it just pays to clear up the confusion as to what the term link baiting actually covers. Link baiting does include both organic and inorganic methods for obtaining links. Inorganic methods are more purposeful and targeted and are often part of a wider campaign. Because link baiting is somewhat new in mainstream Internet media people tend to misunderstand the concept. Link baiting is a more natural way of getting links however it is a broad term for a lot of practices that are both organic and inorganic.

Organic linking techniques:

- Building site content, reviews, news, articles, blog, lists, advice
- Outgoing links to related sites, experts, gurus, resources
- Usability enhancements
- Joining communities and networks
- Promoting product or services

Link baiting campaign techniques (inorganic)
- Reciprocal linking – linking to one website from another website with a link back to the original site. Reciprocal links are a common practice for increasing website traffic and can be organized on a courtesy or contractual basis.
- Swapping links – like reciprocal linking, swapping links basically means one website posts a link to another website; the other website also posts a link to the original website.
- Controversial hooks – anything that serves as an enticement is a hook while a controversial hook is any enticement that is controversial, such as an article ridiculing Google or a major online service provider that is likely to draw people to read it.
- Attack hooks – these are a specific type of controversial hooks; the example mentioned above, an article ridiculing Google or another company or individual, is an attack hook.

- PPC – Pay Per Click refers to advertising with the search engines by bidding on a particular keyword phrase or search term used by Internet users related to information on certain niches and sectors.
- Directory submissions – online website directories organize website links into categories and subcategories.
- Consultation – this is a general process of obtaining information. For websites and link baiting, consultations are generally used to review the effectiveness of existing search engine rankings and develop plans for improvement.
- Email campaigns – attract customers by distributing a sales e-mail to potential clients and existing clients.
- Giveaways in exchange for links – make special offers for free products or service in return for which links to your site are posted on their sites.
- False referrals – in link baiting this is practice frowned upon by most. It often involves clicking on your own link or having someone else who's not really interested in your service, clicking on the link to make a referral and boost your rating. Generally this is caught so be careful.

CHAPTER EIGHT – LINKBAITING SPECIALISTS

Professional Services

Internet marketing is a booming industry and one that is inundated with professionals and scam artists alike. SEO is one of the most significant marketing endeavors of our time. Link baiting is the latest in Internet marketing techniques to capture the worldwide community. Naturally as this market avenue becomes more popular experts in the field have emerged to provide professional link baiting services.

Most SEO companies offer some type of link baiting service. What is more interesting however is the emergence of link baiting specialist services. These are professional Internet marketers who specialize in developing and implementing link baiting strategies.

Link baiting can be a time consuming process and if you don't know what you are doing that time spent could be in vain. A specialist link baiting expert can help with identifying avenues, potential markets and linking opportunities. Much like an SEO specialist a link baiting specialist knows the ins and outs of search engine optimization and how link baiting can work alongside and enhance SEO campaigns.

So what are the benefits of using a link baiting service?

- Link baiting is an approved white hat SEO method.
- A link baiting service will increase natural incoming links with relevant related sites and blogs.
- Natural incoming links are good for SEO.
- Increased traffic, the rate of visitors could literally explode exponentially.
- Increased exposure for your site and brand.
- Targeted, market focussed baiting is a huge benefit. The right visitors translate into conversions.
- A link baiting service will ideally provide development for tech tools and content writing services.
- These types of services manage link baiting campaigns from concept to completion meaning you can get on with what you do best.

What can you expect from a link baiting service?

- The initial phase will generally include industry specific concept design. That is the consultant will come up with a variety of ideas for link bait relating to your distinct business. This part of the process is interactive, as you will be presented with ideas for approval before moving onto the development and implementation.

- Next is the development stage. The specialist will write, create, program or design the link bait.

- Once you have release the bait on your site or blog the company will monitor the progress with a specified time frame.

- The link baiting campaign may include site submissions, promotion, contact with webmasters, bloggers and experts. All contact will be personally customized.

- Regular updates and reports are usually part of the service as well as directory submissions.

Considerations

The outcomes of link baiting campaigns vary in terms of return on investment. The range of return is hard to predict which makes the high initial cost somewhat risky. There are no fixed results so there are no guarantees you will see a ROI in the same range as the next guy.

You may consider a service that provides link baiting as a complement to SEO. There is a growing number of SEM companies that have adopted link baiting as part of their services. SEM specialists will look at the whole package and how they can effectively optimize your site to increase rankings. Link popularity is valuable for maximizing search engine rankings.

So what are the benefits of an SEO link baiting service?

- The number one benefit is that this approach covers all your bases. This type of service will optimize you site holistically. Link bait development is part of the package.
- Good content, clean code and usability features.
- Optimized site content and brand.
- Optimized keywords, phrases and placement
- Increased traffic

What can you expect?

- Initially an SEO will assess current positioning, content, markets and avenues for optimizing your site.

- The whole process will look at many factors including design, coding, links, and content and branding.

- Some services will recommend directions whereas others will manage the whole process including development and design of site, branding, content, link baiting etc.

- Finally they will manage the implementation of submissions, link baiting, directory submissions, article submissions and any other directives they might be taking.

Considerations

Not all SEM companies will have specialized knowledge of link bait techniques. Link baiting sits on the horizon of SEO. At present it is a complementary element to SEO. Companies which specialize specifically in SEO will have good knowledge of link baiting practice simply because it has always been a part of optimization. A link baiting specialist is better suited for companies who want to go above and beyond overall optimization and explore ways to make their link popularity skyrocket. The truth is however as link popularity improves so will rankings and this is a central aim of SEO.

LINK BAITING EXPERTS

As far as link baiting specialists go there are a number of key figures that have emerged as leaders in the industry. These SEM experts have been practicing link baiting for years. In the last year link bait has become a hot topic and the number of resources available has increased exponentially. Leader experts in this area offer link baiting services that can literally turn your business around.

The Leading Experts.

- Eric Ward

Eric Ward is a leading link baiting expert. Ward has been developing linking strategies since 1994 making him one of the most experienced and accomplished link specialists around.

- Andy Hagan

Andy Hagan is a link building and SEO specialist, an established web writer and accomplished expert speaker. Andy has been in the SEO and link building game since 1999 and has developed his strategies with years of knowledge and marketing experience behind him. Hagan also provides specialist link baiting services.

- Aaron Wall

Aaron blog site SEObook.com is one of the most comprehensive resources online for SEO and link bating. SEObook began as a news blog for the latest in search news and information. The blog has now evolved and focuses on providing sound marketing tips, SEO articles and link building ideas. Wall also contributes to popular search news blog www.treadwatch.org.

- Nick Wilson

Nick Wilson was one of the first to coin the term link baiting in an article post on his blog. Wilson is a professional blogger and linking baiting expert. He co-founded the popular blog community performancing.com. His article on linking hooks is recognized as one of the best hook guides available.

- Rand Fish

Rand Fish is a co-founder and CEO of Internet marketing site and blog SEOmoz.org. This site offers comprehensive SEO support and services including extensive information on link baiting. Rand has been developing marketing strategies on the Internet since 1993. Rand and the team at SEOmoz are experts in SEO and Internet marketing and are leaders in the industry.

- Jim Westergren

Jim Westergren is an SEO expert and philosopher. His expert articles can be found online on various popular blogs. Jim's own blog is a great resource for link baiting ideas and SEO advice.

He was one of the primary bloggers responsible for bringing link baiting as an all-encompassing concept into the mainstream.

Corporate Examples

In theory link bait can turnaround your business and increase your businesses potential. Link bait can expand your market, increase your ranking and get people talking about your site. In theory link baiting is a key tool in Internet marketing that can be the difference between site success and failure. Theory is great but not without results to back it up.

Here are some successful linking baiting ideas that have received a lot of attention.

- Behr is a paint store with a great piece of link bait that has taken their site to the next level. Behr's ColorSmart tool allows visitors to select color schemes online in order to see how they would work for specific projects.

- Rand Fish's Page Strength Tool is a good example of corporate link bait. This is a tool related specifically to the concept of SEO so it makes sense that it gets a lot of attention. This specific tool attracts long term ongoing links in the thousands.

- Polartec came up with a great gimmick to promote their product and bait links. Shave Your Yeti is a great concept, with a humorous interactive hook that attracts links and promotes the product. This was a highly successful piece of link bait.

- Google's Matt Cutts is an SEO whose blog articles attract a lot of link love. In particular Cutts 21 Great SEO tips. This was a simple but highly effective piece of link bait.

- The Zug Viagra Prank is an example of a humor hook that skyrocketed. This was a great piece of link bait because it was controversial and humorous. The site was founded in 1995 and has an extensive archive of pranks performed. The most recognized pranks include the viagra prank, the Turnpike Prank, the all Natural Prank and the Credit Card Prank.

- Onion News produced a great piece of link bait with controversial news story the Evangelical Scientists Refute Gravity with New 'intelligent' Falling Theory. This caused uproar in the community and resulted in a big increase in exposure and links.

- A classic piece of link bait that caught the global community was the coke and mentos fountain. This piece of bait was distributed by eepybird.com and attracted significant attention

- Aaaron Wall and Andy Hagan produced a simple but highly effective piece of bait on their blog SEObook. Their 101 ways to link popularity in 2006 article received an extraordinary response in the SEO community and helped to bring link baiting into the mainstream.

CHAPTER NINE – THE BLOGOSPHERE

The Blogosphere – From Diary to Domination

What is now known as the blogosphere began as a simple diary entry on a website. The earliest forms of blogging were personal online journals, chronicles and dairies. Originally they came in the form of email lists and bulletin boards. In the early 90s basic forum software allowed for greater interactivity. Early forms of blogging were interest pages, personal commentary and online dairies.

The modern blog is an extension of the online journal or web log. This began as a personal form of individualized expression. Early journalists would keep a running commentary of their personal lives that was publicly available for feedback. Webmasters also began hosting news sections and updates on their sites. The earliest web logs were simply extensions of already existing sites. As more advanced and easily accessible software became available for hosting thread articles the modern form was born.

Blogs today are a universal phenomenon connecting millions of online publishers. What began, as a simple form of personal expression is now a globally commercial industry. The term web log was coined by Jorn Barger an America blogger in 1997. Peter Merholz shortened the term in 1999.

Blogs really began to boom with the emergence of blog hosting sites where people could publish their writing online and customize their own blog pages. These sites also made it possible to link to other blogs within the network. This meant a significant rise in the interconnectivity of the blogosphere. Web log search engines also helped to connect bloggers to others with similar interests.

By 2001 blogs were a well-established medium for communication across a broad spectrum of subjects. Blogs were also emerging as a news source covering all manner of political and social commentary. Established journalists, politicians, writers and broadcasters began to use blogs.

In recent years blogs have well and truly infiltrated the mainstream, becoming a primary source for news, information, resources and commercial advertising. Blogs have also been adopted by other news mediums and are used by some of the most established broadcasting houses in the world. BBC news has a blog for its editors and The Guardian features daily blog entries. Political campaigns are now commonly using blogs to reach audiences and influence their public.

In 1999 Brad L. Graham coin the term blogosphere referring to the connection of blog communities. Blogs are so effective because they connect people. In this way blogs are great for businesses because they provide an avenue for connection with related businesses and customers alike. Blogs provide multiple opportunity for linking to these businesses and for reaching an extended audience of potential customers.

Blog posts spread like a virus across the blogosphere, which make them ideal for any business trying to spread the word. Link baiting is one concept that blogging brought into the mainstream. Link baiting really became visible within blogging communities as the interactivity made it an ideal scenario for attracting links. Bloggers share links, post comments, post entries and share information. Link baiting is a natural element in the world of blogging.

The blogosphere is now a commercialized industry with many full time bloggers. As the medium continues to grow so to do the networks and connections. Ultimately that is what blogging is all about. Making a connection with like-minded people, reaching an audience of interested parties and sharing information with the global community.

Blogosphere - The Evolution of Link Baiting

Webmasters have been baiting links for as long as there have been commercialized pages on the net. Links are like an intricate navigation system that helps users and search engines work their way around the Internet. Search engines follow links from one page to the next and from site to site. It makes sense then that webmasters would seek to find ways to increase the amount of sites linking to their pages. The more links you have the more visible you are to both users and engines.

The practice of creating natural links is as old as the net itself, so when did it appear in the mainstream? When did the techniques and tricks used by webmasters for years become link baiting? The term itself first began to appear on SEO blogs in the blogosphere. In the last few years blogs have become the way of the World Wide Web. Blogs quickly became commercialized and mainstream. Link baiting practices were especially essential for bloggers trying to reach a large audience in order to cash in on their advertising.

So began the blogophere link baiting phenomenon. In terms of blogging link baiting meant creating content that was so interesting, scandalous, shocking, useful or contrary other bloggers would put a link on their blog. The modern link bait boom began with bloggers writing articles with the specific goal of attracting links to their blog.

Blogs are all about creating communities of like-minded people with common interests. Commercially these kinds of communities are a gold mine. For a business establishing communities means potential customers and networks for increasing business. Blogs offer that opportunity because they are so interactive.

In a very short space of time blogs became a viable income earner with advertising reaching news heights. As the potential for earning increased so to did the link baiting drive. This is where blogs crossed over and became a highly effective marketing tool. Many thriving businesses now have their own blogs for link baiting and marketing purposes. Whereas in the beginning blogging was a form of expression it is now a thriving commercial avenue.

Blogs are one of the most effective ways to link bait because they are so interactive. Blogs are a great avenue for viral marketing, which is essentially what link baiting is. Because blogs are so interconnected within specific communities you have the potential to reach thousands of industry related people.

Nick Wilson first used the term link baiting in a blog entry in 2005. Less than a year later the term returns almost 6 million hits on google. Nick's blog was well established and he was a recognized leader in the SEO field but still the results could not have been predicted.

That is the power of the Internet and of the blogophere, one good idea that can turn global. This is simply because blogging communities are so interconnected. Bloggers and web publishers read and reference other blogs in their own community, they comment on and post for other blogs essentially shrinking the global community. Link baiting exploded into the mainstream with the rise of commercialized blogging communities.

CHAPTER TEN – THE FUTURE OF LINK BAITING

A Vision for the Future

Link baiting is here to stay for the long term. Unlike other Internet trends that have come and gone in the past, link baiting remains fundamental to Internet and SEO marketing. Links are still the primary connectors of the web; they are the navigation system for both users and search engines. Link baiting is an established form of attracting visitors and increasing rankings. In the future link baiting will remain a key Internet marketing tool.

In the past SEO marketing concentrated on keyword density and exchanging links. This was effective for its time but in terms of current SEM these things alone are redundant. The reason link baiting has become so important is because it is actually a very productive form of marketing. Link baiting effectively has a dual impact that past SEM has lacked. This kind of marketing forces you to create something new and unique. It forces you to appeal to your users in a way that has never been done before.

The fact that link baiting is targeted specifically towards users and indirectly towards search engines makes it different from other forms of Internet marketing. Webmasters have in the past geared their SEO campaigns primarily towards search engines. Campaigns included keywords, design and coding techniques. A link baiting campaign is completely audience specific. The bait is not for search engines but for users. This difference suggests link baiting is here to stay in the long term. Search engines approve and encourage link baiting techniques for the most part because generally speaking they enhance the web.

The other major contributing factor to this is the current http protocol. Until this protocol is replaced links will continue to be the connective fiber of the Internet's pages. Search algorithms will still place great importance on link popularity. Backlinks are one of the most important considerations in most search engines ranking assessments. Because of this link baiting looks set to stay at the forefront of SEM.

Link baiting is a unique form of Internet marketing. Although it has been around for a number of years now there is still new ground being forged everyday. Its appeal both to users and search engines is largely due to the fact that link bait benefits the Internet as a whole. This is one of the reasons link bait will remain a mainstream influence in Internet marketing for a long time to come.

So what does the future hold? Link bait is perhaps one of the most lasting trends ever seen in the history of the commercialized web. If you look back at its colorful history it is clear to see that what we call link bait others call viral marketing, what we call an attack hook others call a publicity stunt. The idea of creating something that will get people talking is not new and will properly never grow old. The interesting thing is however the potential of link bait comparatively. A good piece of link bait can reach the world in the blink of an eye. This simply serves to make the world a whole lot smaller. In this way link bait will remain in its various forms a constant connector of the world and the web.

Link Bait – Where it's been and where it's going?

Link bait rocketed into the mainstream in record time. Less than a year after the term started appearing in blogs the concept was global. Millions jumped on the baiting bandwagon, either doing it or talking about it, most likely both. With all the talk and action going on around the area of link baiting it begs the question where is this going?

Fundamentally any piece of good content, useful information or news story can be considered link bait. Many webmasters believe that anything of this nature is nothing more than an attempt at link bait. People are catching on to this and questioning the organic definition. How do you distinguish between something that is the genuine article and something that is genuinely just a piece of link bait? The truth is this is another big gray area.

The question is how will link bait look in the future. Is it set to become another SEO scam? It is well known that back links are great for search engine rankings. It is also known that people will go to extreme lengths to raise their rankings. Genuine link bait is not just another SEO scam. Genuine link bait is something that contributes to the productiveness and relevance of the Internets pages.

In the future it will be hard to know whether a webmasters latest advice or news is just an attempt to boost their popularity. It will be unclear as to whether a content optimized site is just another SEM marketing ploy. The good thing is about link bait, and the thing that will help this trend to endure is that it won't matter if its link bait or not. Good link bait is based on strong content, so the user benefits regardless of the webmasters aim.

It is that simple but fundamental fact that will see link baiting techniques endure and the Internet grow. Link bait is good for the development of our information and lifestyle networks. Link bait has both online implications and offline effects. The world of the Internet intermingles with the literal world.

As for the future of the Internet. It can only be enhanced by the rise of link baiting. Link bait forces webmasters and marketer to consider the audience before the search engines. Link bait inspires creativity, innovation and connection. Connectivity is the ultimate direction of the Internet. Links not only connect pages but people, networks, businesses and communities. At present these online communities are growing and in the future these communities will be the face of the Internet.

So the challenge for the future is to create bait that is more than bait. The best approach to this is to look at the holistic health of your site and business. Start from the inside out and as you do create bait that reflects the essence of what you have to offer. Bait for the sake of bait is a big hit right now but in the future link bait will have to be even more creative. The trick will be going beyond a singular piece of bait to a whole site of bait. The bait will need to be more focussed on specific audiences rather than the general web public.

Overall the future looks good for link bait and for the growth and development of web communities. Link bait is very simply just another way to connect to the external world. Only this type of connection is designed to elicit a very specific response, a back link.

Web Communities

The earliest conception of the Internet was formed out of need for a more effective communications medium. The very basic primary functions of the Internet were based around simple forms of communicating. The idea of communication is still a central theme when it comes to the modern web. Sure the forms and functions of the Internet have evolved beyond recognition of that original template, but the idea is the same. The Internet both in its commercial form and otherwise is about communication. That is communicating information, branding, marketing and commerce.

The web is no longer made up of individual sites and pages existing on a singular network. The web is an intricate weaving of communities, industries and networks. The Internet is driven by the natural linking of millions of pages. Without links web pages would exist in a vacuum. Links are the natural fibers that connect the world of web pages. These connections are both internal and external.

It is the external links that have the greatest implications for the future of the web. That future consists of intricate communities. Already the phenomenal emergence of the blogosphere has taken the world of web communities to another level. Blogs are an example of where the Internet is heading. Natural linking is the simplest form of a web community. The simple act of referencing another site or blog creates a community environment. This is most visible in industry specific communities and interest specific communities. Links bring together like-minded individuals to form a communicating community.

Link baiting originated as a technique with the specific purpose of getting other webmasters to link to a site. The more links acquired the greater your community of networks and your visibility. Link baiting started as a drive to connect with other members of an industry in order to drive specific traffic to the site. The face of link baiting now is a commercial one. The spin off of this is increased link popularity and therefore ranking. Link baiting has fallen into the SEO category in many ways. It has been validated as a certified SEM technique.

Link baiting is now a major consideration in SEO campaigns. This has a number of implications. It further develops the need for communities and connections and it enhances link baiting techniques and strategies. Link bait is not something solely used by bloggers within web communities it is now used by corporations, big brands and SME's.

Communication is an ever-changing industry. The mediums by which we achieve effective communication have diversified and developed over the years into something that no one could have predicted. Whether by accident, purpose, link bait or SEO communities have emerged as the new medium for communications. Blogging communities, business communities and the like are the new face of the Internet.

ONLINE RESOURCES

The term link bait results in 5,920,000 search hits on google. That's a lot of information to sort through and a lot of resources at your fingertips. This is an overwhelming number to comprehend but it gives you an idea as to how many people are talking about link bait right now. The term itself has literally spread like a virus across the search engines invading every Internet marketing, SEO and SEM page. People can't get enough of link baiting.

Here are some of the top sites and blogs dedicated to SEO and Link baiting.

Link Baiting and SEO resources

- Nick Wilson's blogging community - http://performancing.com/node/38

- Aaron Wall's SEO blog – http://www.seobook.com

- A journal of search engine news - http://www.searchenginejournal.com/?p=2797

- Rand Fish's SEO blog – http://www.SEOmoz.com

- Jim Westergren's blog – http://www.jimwestergren.com

- Small business guide to search engines - http://ww.searchengineguide.com

- SEM news site - http://searchenginewatch.com/showPage.html?page=3623287

- SEO resource - http://www.seoegghead.com/blog/seo/link-bait-and-its-electronic-cousin-p24.html

- News Site - http://www.sitepronews.com/archives/2006/jan/23.html

- Link Building specialists services - http://www.seo-fusion.com/

- Defining Link Bait - http://en.wikipedia.org/wiki/Link_bait

- Search Engine forum - http://forums.searchenginewatch.com/showthread.php?t=2616&page=1

- Eric Ward's site – http://ericward.com

- Various articles - http://www.technorati.com

GLOSSARY

- **Affiliate linking** – Linking with sites that you are affiliated with in your industry or complementary industries.

- **Alexa** – A rank based on website traffic, focuses on SEM and web resources.

- **Article directory** – This refers to directories which host articles. There are both free and paid submission sites.

- **Back links** – These are incoming links from other sites. Link popularity is essential for search engine rankings. The more high quality back links you have the greater your ranking will be.

- **Black Hat** – refers to techniques considered to be search engine ranking manipulation. These techniques generally fall outside the guidelines of search engine etiquette and not considered good SEO practices. Cloaking is an example of a black hat technique.

- **Blog** – Online journal, web log.

- **Blogosphere** – This term encompasses all blogs within a community or social network. The interconnectivity of blogs is a social phenomenon. Bloggers read, comment on and link to other blogs within their community making it high interactive.

- **Content** – Web content refers to copy including articles, lists, resources, references blogs, advertising, interviews and information. Good content makes great link bait.

- **Click through rate** – The rate of click through compared to the rate of link views. This is calculated as a percentage.

- **Cloaking** – This is a nasty search engine manipulation technique that involves tricking the search engine into recording content on the URL that differs from what the user will see. There are many technical ways this can be achieved and there are circumstances where search engine will approve cloaking methods for paid submissions.

- **Crawler** – Just like a spider a crawler scans pages on the Internet and indexes them in the search engine database.

- **Complementary site** – refers to sites that provide complementary products or services to your own or sites that are valuable to your users.

- **del.icio.us** – Tech site that bookmarks pages.

- **DMOZ** – Searches google and shows how many sites and pages are listed in the DMOZ directory

- **.edu Link** – Shows how many .edu links are pointing to a site. (Yahoo)

- **.gov Link** – Shows how many .gov links are pointing to a site. (Yahoo)

- **Guru** – An expert is a particular field.

- **Keywords** – The search terms webmasters use in their content and coding to help the search engine match the site with relevant searches. Strong keywords are essential for search engine rankings.

- **Link Bait** –refers to anything that is put on a site that generates incoming links from other sites. Link bait can include content, downloads, resources, online tools or literally anything else that encourages back links. Link bait is important for link popularity, which helps determine a sites search, engine ranking.

- **Link baiting** – refers to link bait techniques used to generate incoming links. Link baiting is a natural form of building back links however it can also be a purposeful marketing ploy.

- **Link building** – refers to obtaining outside links in order to increase direct click through and search engine ranking.

- **Link popularity** – refers to a site's numerical incoming links. The more links the site has the more popular it is. Link popularity is an assessment made by search engines when ranking a site.

- **Link baiting specialist** – A specialized service that specifically designs link bait and manages link bait campaigns.

- **Link trading** – refers to the practice of trading links with other sites. This is a mutually beneficial arrangement that works best when the sites are related or complementary in some way.

- **Meme** – Something made by a webmaster that others can replicate or use but that links back to the origin.

- **Natural links** – This refers to links that are generated naturally. Link bait in its basic forms is considered natural linking.

- **Organic links** – These are natural links attracted by site content and value.

- **Outbound links** – Links on a page that leads to another page either within the site or external to the site.

- **Page hit** – This refers to the retrieval of any content, graphics or pages from a web server. Page hits are not an accurate indicator of actual site visits; every component of the site is recorded as an independent hit.

- **Page Rank**– This google patent refers to the relevance and importance of a page as determined by the search engine. Link popularity, keyword connections and content relevance are all influential factors in a pages ranking.

- **Page view** – This refers to a singular visit to a web page by a human visitor. This is a good indicator of actual visits and is commonly used for advertising purposes.

- **Permalink** – This is a word associated primarily with blogging but is also used in other web applications. A permalink is a link that connects to a blog entry even after the entry has been removed from the front page. This kind of link remains indefinitely unchanged.

- **Podcast** – a multimedia file transmitted via the Internet for use on mobile devices or personal computers.

- **Reciprocal linking** – refers to placing a link on a site in exchange for a reciprocal link. This is more effective than simply requesting links.

- **ROI** – Return on Investment

- **Search Engine fodder** – Content designed solely for the search engine that serves no purpose for human audiences.

- **SEM** – Search engine marketing refers to the techniques used by webmasters to drive traffic to their sites via search engine rankings.

- **SEO** – Search engine optimization refers to the techniques used by webmasters to optimize their sites to increase their search engine rankings. Optimization fundamentals include strong keywords, good content, clean design and effective link bait.

- **Search engine ranking** – This refers to the ranking given to a site by the search engine. This is reflected in the search results. The top ten results are considered prime real estate for a site.

- **Search engine submission** – This refers to the act of submitting a site to a search engines index. This is only necessary if a major search engine has not picked up the site.

- **Search hit** – Any time your search criteria matches pages or content in the search engines index. Search results are often referred to as hits.

- **SME** – Small to medium sized enterprises

- **Site Directory** – directories are sites that you can submit links to in order to increase exposure and visibility. There are both free and paid directories. These directories are man made search engine indexes.

- **Spam** – This refers to techniques that are detrimental to the ability of the search engine to provide relevant, authentic results. Spam comes in many forms and every search engine has varying guidelines. Spam includes, overloaded keyword content that makes no sense to a human audience, gateway pages made only for search engines, unsolicited email campaigns and much more.

- **Spiders** – A search engine spider is software program designed to crawl and index pages on the Internet. The spider crawls the page and links from one page to the next. Spider software is designed as a ranking tool and database for search engines.

- **Technorati** – Estimates the total number of incoming links from blogs to a site.

- **Traffic** – Visitors to a page or site.

- **Tools** – refers to something useful and usable on a site. Examples of tools include a mortgage calculator, body mass indicator, currency converter or calorie counter.

- **Usability** – refers to the ease at which a user can perform tasks on a site, navigate, find relevant information and achieve their goals on the site. Usability techniques are about creating an improved user experience. A user-friendly site is appealing to both audience and engines.

- **White Hat** – refers to natural traffic drives and natural linking techniques such as content building and site quality. White hat SEO techniques are search engine approved.

www.ingramcontent.com/pod-product-compliance
Lightning Source LLC
Chambersburg PA
CBHW071116210326
41519CB00020B/6324

9 789810 808822